I0469618

40 Ways 2 Win In Business

The 'Starting Level' Book in the Ways 2 Win series giving Hints and Tips about Business Techniques, Human Resources, Customer Care and a Winning Philosophy.

John H Lightfoot

of South Shields

40 Ways 2 Win In Business

The first in a series of books written by
John Lightfoot
On Ways 2 Win in Business, Marketing and Exporting.

Especially useful as a *Travellers Companion*.

DEDICATION

This, my very first book, is dedicated to my wife Lilian, who has never been able to understand why I get so much pleasure out of my work, whatever it happens to be and why my work is also my hobby.

However we have remained happily married since 1967, especially after I realised a successful marriage is based on 2 simple words, "Yes Dear!"

ABOUT THE AUTHOR

John Lightfoot began his career as a Marine Engineer Cadet with Shell Tankers and was immediately enthralled by the joys and excitement of travel. After 9 years he left the sea and worked for a year with RCA as a Maintenance Supervisor, 5 years as a Hospital Engineer then a spell as the Factory Manager of a window blind manufacturing company based in his South Shields home town. It was during his time in the factory, in 1974 that many of the self employed agents would call to pick up their orders and regale to John how great things were and how exciting and rewarding it was being self-employed.

Motivated to become one of them but scared of not being able to sell, John was assured that the products 'sold themselves, and with most agents having shops in or very near to a town's high street, only a minimum of selling skills were needed.

After a year of managing the factory, the agency for Sunderland became available for a fee of £1,800, probably equivalent to around £20,000 at 2013 prices. Realising he would need some additional funds to refurbish the Sunderland showroom, buy a van so he could go round measuring and fitting and support the family in case the business needed time to become profitable, John and his wife Lilian agreed to re-mortgage their home for £3,000 and hope for the best.

Because there was sufficient equity in their house, their solicitor was on the board of the Building Society, the accountant they were going to appoint for their business needs (recommended by their solicitor) was also on the board of the Building Society and the previous owner's accounts for the new business showed it was profitable enough to make the repayments, there was no need for John to produce a Business Plan. In fact he opened the bank account for his business and traded for the first 15 months without ever seeing the bank manger, until the funds dried up and he needed to go into an overdraft situation.

So no Business Plan was required, there was nobody to talk to about the highs and lows of the business, close friends who were in business kept advising against employing people and John lacked any real business experience, thinking that if he just kept working hard it will all come together. It was not a good start and many things should have been done differently.

ABOUT THE AUTHOR continued

Having established his business in 1975 and still being in control of it today, John has had plenty of time to put right all of the mistakes he made initially but also to build on some the things he got right from the very start.

After 38 years running his own organisation he has seen it all, done it all and has collected over 20 business and export awards on the way.

As a result of building up a brand leading product that is well known and respected throughout the global marine industry and a customer service that is equally as impressive to go with it, the highlight of John's remarkable career was to be invited to Buckingham Palace in 2002 and presented with the MBE by Her Majesty Queen Elizabeth II during her Golden Jubilee year, for Services To International Trade. It was to be capped 10 years later when John and Lilian were again invited to Buckingham Palace to witness daughter Julie being honoured in exactly the same way, this time during Her Majesty's Diamond Jubilee year.

Julie works in the family business as Managing Director, with John as Chairman and for the business to have been honoured once was a great achievement but twice in the same family just proves how extra special this guy, his family, his people and his organisation really is. On display in the Board Room at Solar Solve there are over 20 awards for exports, Investors in People, good business practice and Excellence in the Marine Industry.

Readers will know that being a winner is not going to be easy and that buying this book is just the start. In fact it will be the easiest part of the whole process. How you will benefit from the book is by reading and learning in a couple of hours what John has learned in almost 40 years of self employment and has been applying very successfully for more than 20 years, to turn his ailing business into a world wide winning enterprise

If anyone can give you hints, tips, advice and the benefit of experience on how best to start up a winning business or turn an existing business into a winner it has to be John Lightfoot.

Read on, enjoy, apply and reap the rewards.

PREFACE

I began writing chapters for a business book back in 2005 when I was asked by the local Business Club to give a presentation on Sales and Marketing and thereafter to write a short column for the Weekly Business Page in the local Shields Gazette.

I got somewhat carried away, writing far more than was required and decided that a Business Book might be a good idea.

At the time my company was becoming too big for the premises in which it was located and so we decided to relocate to a new purpose built factory that had almost 4 times the floor space.

Because I wanted to be totally involved in the planning, execution and aftermath of the move, the book writing was put aside until later. The relocation took 9 months in all, of total commitment to the task but it was worth the effort because it was completed without any disruption to customer service. But then we had to concentrate all of our efforts on winning more orders to grow the business and expand into all of the extra space we were committed to renting – for the next 10 years.

The world wide recession didn't help matters but we got there eventually. Then as we began winning Export and Business Awards once more and people were complimenting us and congratulating me on how well run and successful my business was, I was motivated to go back to this book to explain to anyone interested, that it really is not so difficult. Certainly it takes a lot of hard work and dedication but in the early years, during my not-very-successful business life I was working hard and was very dedicated but didn't earn much money and put in a whole lot more hours every week than I needed to as we began to improve.

I am a Chartered Engineer and Fellow of the Institute of Marine Engineers, which gave me a good grounding in both practical experiences and academic achievement. I have been both Chairman and Marketing Director of Solar Solve Ltd since its formation in 1988 and in 2005 attained a Diploma in Company Direction, awarded by the Institute of Directors. I am a Fellow of South Shields Marine School at South Tyneside College, where I gained all of my sea-going training, education and qualifications.

Although I am now a manufacturer; for the first 18 years of my self employment I ran a town centre window blind showroom and so, all-in-all, I think I have something worthwhile to offer anyone who is already involved in business or thinking about it.

INTRODUCTION

A winning business owner, entrepreneur or whatever other name you care to choose, will need to be familiar and adept at many skills and will have to execute a whole host of winning strategies.

Absolutely none of them require you to have the skills of a brain surgeon as they are all just common sense. There is no mystique. All you need is the will to survive, the determination to win, the application to ensure everything that should happen does happen and the discipline to oversee the whole operation personally.

The only other requirement is a tool to guide you. You will find within the pages of *40 Ways 2 Win In Business* most, if not all of the advice necessary to get a new business up and running or to turn an existing business into a winner.

The author has tried to keep the advice flowing in a logical sequence of how events will occur for a business that is being newly established and consequently in what order, more or less, the different aspects and procedures for creating or improving your business will be required as time goes by.

For the readers who run established businesses and are looking to improve them, which should be all of them of course, the chapters are readily identifiable by their Titles, have a short precise about the subject in the shaded Intro-Box and are individualised to cover that subject only.

Finally, the last paragraph of many chapters will suggest seeking impartial advice from Service Providers, which can often be free.

To save printing a long paragraph at these locations throughout this book I will give a fully expanded definition here and in chapter 3 only. Thereafter only a brief sentence will be used.

In most towns and cities there are local government agencies and council backed organisations that are set up to help owners and managers of small and medium sized businesses with free advice on all aspects of business operation. Staff at the local Chamber of Commerce in your area are also usually ready to help with some good advice or by just listening to your concerns. You may be surprised just how much help there is available and usually initial consultations are FREE.

The *40 Ways 2 Win* series covers all of the strategies you will need and gives you some hints and tips about what sort of further help you should be requesting from Service Providers.

CONTENTS

If you are thinking of starting a business you need to check through 5WH - What? Why? Who? Where? When? How? What will you offer and Why? Who will be your customers and Where will they be located? When will it begin and How will it all happen?

The following notes contain the bullet points only. Each heading is a whole issue all of its own that has to be addressed and successfully overcome. Working through them to achieve your ultimate objective will be exciting, stressful, satisfying and hopefully profitable.

001 - What? Why? Who? Where? When? How?

What?

Nobody should set up in business to sell a product until they have convinced themselves and all around them that there is a market for it. The product or service is **What** you are going to supply.

Why?

A first response to this is usually along the lines of "because there was a gap in the market and I foresaw a great opportunity to do something about it".

That's all fine and dandy for hobbyists. I would suggest that the real reason **Why** most entrepreneurs set up in business is usually to make money for themselves. I always think it is nice that in doing this we also make people (usually customers) happy or better still, delighted to have dealt with us.

Who?

Where are the customers for this great product going to come from? What is the target market? Who will buy it? A good deal of 'In Depth Market Research' will need to be properly carried out to find the answer to this question. This is possibly the most important question to answer. Do not go ahead with anything else until you have done this and established to the very best of your ability **Who** will buy your product or service.

Where?
This is a double-edged question. Where to work from and Where to sell to?

Will you need a shop, office, or just work from home and what area of your locality will you need to be based?

Where will your target market be located? Will you service enquiries and deal with customers locally, nationally or internationally? It may be that you want to tread with caution at first and leave international work until you are established.

Where from and **Where** to are very important.

When?
Getting the launch date right will almost certainly be crucial to the initial success of your venture. If there is anything seasonal about the product or service set your strategy accordingly and always aim for some days, weeks or months before the optimum launch date. Depending on how many imponderables have to be overcome this may need to be extended further. If there will be periods of exceptional demand followed by long stretches of virtual inactivity, **When** to open for business will be a few weeks early rather than a few weeks late of the high season.

It is common sense of course but there are always many instances when things go wrong and the new venture can fail because there are no funds available to trade out of a quiet period.

How?
Another two-edged sword. How will it happen and how will the venture succeed?

It has more chance of happening if you take a personal interest and are in control of everything up to and beyond the launch date. It is more likely to succeed if you retain a personal interest and always put your customers first.

Your personal involvement is **How** it will all work..

Stop now and put this book back on the shelf if you are not absolutely and totally committed to Applying yourself and Disciplining yourself to ensure that your business organisation, whatever size it may be, becomes a winner.

If you are not serious about winning then you will need an inordinate amount of Luck to get you there and I am a great believer in the saying 'There is no such thing as Luck. You make your own Luck'.

So get on board and read what you need to do to become a winner and then apply yourself wholeheartedly to doing it.

002 - Application PLUS Discipline Works Wonders

It is possible to apply yourself to creating a winning business and yet for it not to succeed, simply because the application may be spasmodic or out of sync with reality. Like virtually all of the qualities listed in this book; application needs to be combined with one or more other qualities, motivational forces or skills to become effective.

All of your tasks, procedures, processes must be carried out totally, fully and with no distractions. When you are doing something either physically or mentally you must give it your full attention to achieve the best result possible.

This philosophy will soon bear dividends that you will be delighted with but because it engenders a whole lot of hard work and concentration you will almost certainly start to look for corners that you can cut, like easier ways to half-do things, that will hopefully gain you the same effective results.

Forget it. The bad news is that it doesn't work like that. There is only one way and that is the hard way. It would be so nice if life was that easy. Just remember though that if it was easy everybody would be doing it and you would not then get the opportunity to stand out from the rest and be a winner.

To be absolutely committed to everything you do is not going to be easy but it is going to be necessary.

That is where the Discipline comes in. We are all impressed when we see groups of people performing at military tattoos, gymnastics displays and especially the Olympic Games, where the best-of-the-best show off their skills to the world at large.

Obviously they all have at least two motivational forces in play; determination and discipline. Whatever it is that you wish to achieve, you are unlikely to be successful without the discipline to see it through.

You don't necessarily have to work as hard physically as Olympic athletes, depending on the kind of organisation you are going to make into a winner but it will be just as demanding in other ways.

The good news is that if you are prepared to apply yourself, all the discipline does is ensure you do it effectively and efficiently so you do not waste your time and energy. It will get you into a routine and a mind-set that will make what you do become a natural way of working and possibly even living because you will be so impressed with what you can do and what you have achieved.

Human nature for a lot of people is to do things quickly, especially busy people, sometimes at the expense of accuracy or perfection. There is nothing wrong with the practice of fast working but there is if the end results are slip-shod in any way.

Human nature for some other people is taking whatever time is necessary to achieve perfection in whatever it is they are doing. There is nothing wrong with this outlook on life either and of the two, this is probably the better type of person to create a winning enterprise because perfection is the objective, albeit in an extended time frame.

My view is that to be winners we should apply ourselves to achieving perfection but discipline ourselves to realise that some customers are going to want it sooner rather than later and so have processes in place to make it happen for them.

Business Partnerships come in a variety of forms and sizes. From working to sleeping and from small family loans to multi million pound venture capital deals. Often there is no money involved just an agreement to work together towards a common aim. Over time however, that could deteriorate into an argument that it was more of a loosely defined arrangement, rather than a hard and fast agreement and that the original aim has veered off-course. If this is an area that interests you, be warned that there must be tens, if not hundreds of thousands of cases where great friends have entered into business partnership agreements and ended up hating one another. Partnerships can be very beneficial but need a great deal of understanding!

003 - Business Partnerships

Business partnerships come in many guises including...

Individuals who join your organisation as a Partner or Director to work with you, giving practical help and support for a share of the business itself, be it Sole Trader, Firm or Limited Company.

Financial business partnerships by way of Bank Loans, Venture Capitalists, Business Angels or Private Investors.

You may have a small business, doing very well, maybe even 1 or 2 employees. It could be a new business or 10 years old, you can still face the same dilemma, "I am hampered by lack of cash for investment to expand and I could also do with someone I can talk to. Someone who understands what it is all about and with whom I can share my vision as well as my frustrations".

Many business partnerships and joint directorships fail because one person feels that he or she works harder and puts more into the business than the other(s). There are also many successful partnerships, however it is not always easy to find people who can work well together.

Similarly with financial partnerships. Sometimes bringing into a business a financier who has the additional skills that are required to lead and direct the organisation can be the solution that turns a struggling small firm into a thriving big company.

Partners need to be adequately rewarded for their contribution. They are working for money just as you are and are certainly less likely to be working for love. If the business is your baby you may be motivated for reasons other than money but most of the people around you, whilst wanting the business to do well and be a great success, will be committing themselves for the financial rewards. If you keep promising to-morrow then make sure it comes sooner rather than later, or else it may be too late(r).

If you don't want any interference from outsiders then the bank may help or you could consider a private personal investor (PPI) who will invest cash for a portion of the business with very little further input. In this case you need to be happy that a sleeping partner's investment could grow 100 fold or more in a few years time as a result of all your hard work. Be appreciative of the role your silent partner played in the success of the venture because it needed both of you in different ways and you are both reaping the rewards. That is a truly successful partnership.

If you fail to give adequate thought and consideration to this subject and then go down the road of creating a partnership with someone or some organisation, then you will suffer the consequences. Indeed you will still have to suffer any consequences if you give it weeks of thought, but the extra time taken will prevent you from rushing in and accepting anything that is offered. For example you may be able to negotiate a better deal from a PPI if you have time to work out something better structured towards a greater reward for yourself if you will be doing all of the work.

Business partnerships need to be approached with great caution and only after you have sought some impartial advice and had a good discussion with your accountant who will no doubt have lots of stories to tell you. Local service providers are also definitely worth approaching for free initial advice and assistance.

Owners and managers of start-up businesses, or existing businesses that are looking for funding, often write Business Plans, usually covering the first 3 years, on the insistence of their professional advisers and / or the people who are being asked to finance the venture. Very often, once the venture is up and running the 3-year plan is forgotten about and progress continues on a wing and prayer. Quite literally it is forgotten about, having been used only as a required tool to launch the venture, when it should still retain tremendous value as a consultative document to help drive the organisation forward. Established successful organisations value the benefits of a 3-year plan and will always be working with one.

004 – Business Plans

Although by no means vital to the success of running or managing a business organisation, it certainly is good practice and indeed sound common sense to have a plan of how you expect your establishment to perform in the next 1 to 3 years.

It is now considered to be a requirement that all organisations should have a 3-year plan as a broad guide to how the owners / directors / managers see their objectives for the future.

Those that are doing the job properly will review the plan annually to ensure that all of the changes in circumstances are taken into consideration and possibly re-plan accordingly. In my business we have a rolling 3-Year Plan that is reviewed, revised and re-written; with a new 3-Year Plan being issued every year. This ensures that the first year of the revised plan is always up to date with its objectives and therefore more likely to be realistic and achievable.

There is another school of thought that a 3-year plan should be just that, based on the premise that you got every prediction for the next 3 years correct when the plan was first written and even if the first year goes awry that does not mean the ultimate 3 year objectives will not be met... so stick with it.

I contend that this attitude is more aligned with laziness and by the end of year 1, with the benefit of hindsight the 3-year targets as laid out in the plan will no longer be ideal. If it is then fine, just leave the plan alone or maybe just tweak it slightly if some part of it can no longer be followed exactly but is still generally in line with your organisation's objectives.

If a few things have changed however and you have the time or resources to rewrite it and it is being used as a useful working tool, then maybe the opportunity should be taken to review it and re-issue a new 3-Year Plan. After all a year is a long time in business.

There really is not much point in writing 3-year plans and then doing nothing about changing them until the 3 years are up. They are possibly better than no plans at all but have questionable real value after about 12 to 18 months, unless your organisation is unique.

There are so many circumstances, situations and imponderables that can affect a manager's plans for the future, such as: legislation, failure to achieve sales targets, unforeseen significant changes in supplier prices including power, political instability, human resources, availability of industrial property, terrorism, competition, overtrading, customer default and non payment for goods / services, oil price increases and so the list goes on.

You will realise therefore, that taking into consideration so many chances of getting it wrong, the statement that someone who can draw up a 3-year plan and get it more or less 'spot on' has to be 'unique'. There are not many of them about, so for the purposes of this exercise you should assume you will not be one of them.

Produce your 3-year plan using your best guess, heavily influenced by lots of research and some good old-fashioned caution.

By all means write lots of words to put meat on the bones and to describe how certain objectives are going to be achieved, including the logical thinking behind it all. You need to document where all the statistics have come from and what research was carried out.

Even if you do not need to borrow funds, it is good discipline to produce a plan that your bank manager or a lender would find acceptable, then it is more likely to be accurate and extremely beneficial to you in your quest to be a winner.

Finally, the words by themselves mean nothing unless there are projections charts or spreadsheets showing turnover and budgets, profit and loss account, balance sheet and cash flow forecasts. All of these tools should be referred to constantly thereafter.

Subjects that should be included in your 3-year plan are:

- Objectives for each of the 3 individual years.
- Strategy For Growth (Or not).
- Where sales will come from and projected annual totals.
- How selling prices have been calculated.
- What the overheads will be.
- What profits are expected.
- Where any funding will come from and how much.
- Where Supplies will come from.
- How many employees will be needed.
- Company Organisation Chart.
- Mission, Vision and Other statements.
- Reference to all Stakeholders.
- A Conclusion

If the Plan includes a requirement to apply for funding then a separate Cash Flow Chart will almost certainly be needed as well.

> *If you have something in mind for your business to help improve it but the costs could become an issue, don't be put off by lack of funds. All types of grants are available, you just have to look for them. Usually a percentage of the full cost is offered but occasionally they are available to cover all of the expenditure. Often they may not amount to much but sometimes they can be significant.*
>
> *One thing is for sure – if you don't investigate grant availability you'll never know what you might be missing, which could be important.*

005 - Business Grants

If you run or manage a small or medium size organization you should not take for granted the fact that if you want to do "something" you will have to pay for it all yourself.

What is included in the "something"? Marketing projects, translation services, HR, travel, hotels, exhibitions, Information and Communication Technology (ICT) hardware and software, business advice, training, Investors in People (IIP), Investors in Excellence (IIE), Quality Assurance, the list goes on.

For most of the above it is possible to receive direct financial assistance towards the cost of any project but you must be able to show that without the grant you would not be able to proceed.

It is a fact that during times of recession, when governments and local councils are forced to make savings, availability of grant funding takes a nose-dive, being a prime target to be cut. However it is not usually eliminated and therefore grants will still be available but to a lesser extent.

The benefits of receiving a grant are obvious and could mean you are able to complete more meaningful Market Research or if you are an exporter, have literature translated into two languages instead of just one for example.

It may be the case that direct financial assistance by way of a cash grant is not available or applicable to a potential project but other types of assistance are. Projects that may come under this category could be staff training including NVQ's, Business Consultancy, IIP, IIE, and Quality Assurance all of which may offer subsidised rates for example.

Some grants are easy to get, to the extent that someone will visit you and complete the necessary documentation as they go through it with you. Staff Training often comes under this category. Other grant applications can be long drawn out affairs with no guarantees at the end of them that you will get anything. You should take this into consideration, especially if you are a small organisation; the monetary reward is going to be small and you are tight on time; or if you intend to pay someone to make the application for you.

Your local government and other service providers exist to help SME's (Small and Medium-sized Enterprises, up to 250 employees) incubate, grow and prosper. Both types of organisation need one and the other. Each project that is submitted will be dealt with on its merit and usually sympathetically whenever possible.

The message is simple. Before you discard an idea because of lack of funds, check with your local service providers to see if they can help directly or advise you of someone who possibly can. It's definitely worth asking because if the service providers don't know about you and what your plans are, then they cannot help.

It's good to talk and even better if you are talking to someone who wants to listen and wants to help. Beware though of the people who get paid for signing you up to a deal which ends up giving you a lot of extra work and form filling, if it will not justify the rewards.

Also realise that with just about any type of grant there will be some ongoing paperwork to complete, often you have to almost prove that you don't need a grant before you can be approved and sometimes the money does not actually come into your bank account for some weeks after all of the approval processes are completed and you have paid for everything in advance.

It seems like 'Turning Adversity Into Opportunity' is a saying I have been hearing all of my life. It has been going on for a long time and I guess on reflection it must have been going on since man first appeared on earth.

So it's nothing new and I raise it only to confirm that it happens in business from time to time and is something that should be looked upon positively at the pre-planning stage.

Winners who are about to set out on their mission to create a winning enterprise are bound to be concerned about things going wrong. Well they do of course, and often it turns out to be good for the organisation, because as a consequence of redressing the issue an opportunity arises that is taken advantage of, which improves the enterprise.

006 - Setbacks Are New Opportunities

We all experience occasional setbacks in just about everything we do and working to create or improve a business organisation will be no exception.

There are two other chapters that refer to setbacks; one comes towards the end of this book and is entitled *'Plan B's – For When Things Go Wrong'* and the other will be in a follow-up book, yet to be written and it will have the title *'Disaster Recovery Planning'.*

In this chapter though I want to put your mind at rest by explaining and convincing you that in most cases, setbacks are just great opportunities to reinvent something, or at least analyse it and make some effective changes for the better.

Even with the best will in the world, a winning business will lapse in some respects and as a consequence the setback ends up being the ideal vehicle to right the wrong.

In this first example your quality system may require you to review all of your suppliers annually, to ensure you are always getting the best deal from them. If you have lots of suppliers it can be a pretty daunting task but if one of them can no longer supply a vital product, you have no option but to get your finger out and start looking for an alternative supplier. You may already have a secondary supplier that you can use in the meantime, whilst doing your research but you will need to find another supplier as you should always have at least two for every product.

I have always though it remarkable that once I start to apply myself to the task, there are usually more alternative choices than I remembered from the last time I did it. It doesn't always work out that the current alternative supplier moves up to the No.1 slot either. However, we usually end up better off as a result.

In 2005, after 12 years on an industrial estate of small 'nursery' factories we had expanded into 4 units and were applying to the local council for a 5th unit. They refused because the units were there to help start-up businesses get established and then move on. We were actually depriving 2 or 3 small businesses access to these 'easy in – easy out' units that are vital to their success.

If we wanted to get bigger, and we did, we needed to find a suitable facility elsewhere, which we did, accidentally through business networking. Our MD was made aware of a factory that would be going up in a few weeks time and less than 2 miles from the current location. It had no tenant and if we acted quickly it would be adapted to suit our requirements as it was being built.

It was still a major decision for us because it had over 3 times the floor space of the current facilities but we would be able to set up a streamlined production flow and benefit from more office space, canteen facilities, car parking and lots of other things. Not least, was the ability to have a fork lift truck, which put an end to a lot of manual handling that was not conducive to an effective Health and Safety policy AND it also saw the demise of staff running between 4 scattered factories in all kinds of weather.

We all started when I was approached by the local Lord Lieutenants Office to see if I would be interested to host a visit to the Solar Solve factory by His Royal Highness The Duke of York, KG, GCVO on a date in June.

Whilst we were honoured and accepted the offer, we were not

too surprised because we had entertained high profile visitors in the past, as a result of the successes and awards the company had been winning since 1996. I had built up a good working relationship with both the local and national officers of the DTI (Department of Trade and Industry), as a result of me always acknowledging the significant help I received from them with my export sales and marketing projects, in subsequent press releases.

We were also winning awards, some of which were sponsored by the DTI and by 2005 I had also been awarded an MBE and invited to a number of other Royal events in London. Anyway, that Royal visit didn't happen because Tony Blair called a General Election and so all Royal visits were cancelled as a matter of course, until a new government was elected.

We moved into our brand new facility in the Port of Tyne at the end of March 2006 and because of my aspirations for the business, I wanted to have an Official Opening that we could be proud of and to gain as much publicity from as possible. For the company and also my home town of South Shields.

I contacted the local Lord Lieutenants Office and asked if Her Majesty The Queen would open the factory next time she was in the area. They replied that Her Majesty didn't open factories but they could arrange for Prince Andrew to open it on his next visit to the North East, which did happen and it was a resounding success.

These are just 3 examples of setbacks that proved to be great opportunities for my company.

Australian MP Michelle O'Byrne, pictured here on the left with Julie and John Lightfoot, visited the old Solar Solve Factory in January 2000 whilst undertaking a fact finding tour of British businesses as a guest of the British Government. She had specifically asked for Solar Solve to be included in her itinerary.

South Shields MP David Miliband was invited to tour Solar Solve's new facility in September of 2006 having previously visited the old factory in 2002. He was very impressed and said, "Solar Solve is a great example of a local firm doing well."

In January 2011 Solar Solve played host to Mr. Michael John (MJ) Holloway OBE, Her Majesty's Ambassador to the Republic of Panama. He was on a fact-finding mission before taking up his new post and wanted to meet owners and managers of businesses that are currently exporting to Panama in particular and South America in general.

On 7th December 2006 HRH The Duke of York KG. KCVO as UK Special Representative for International Trade and Investment, toured Solar Solve's new purpose built facility in the Port of Tyne, South Shields before officially opening it at the end of his visit. Seen here enjoying a joke with John and Lilian Lightfoot, HRH Prince Andrew was accompanied by Nigel Sherlock Esq., Lord-Lieutenant of Tyne & Wear who is also enjoying the joke, in the background.

Solar Solve's brand new 15,000 square foot facility opened for business in March 2006. It is the fourth location since the original business was founded in a town centre showroom in Sunderland in 1975, by husband and wife team John and Lilian Lightfoot, as Northern Window Blind Co.

In 1988 the owners decided to concentrate solely on the manufacture of specialist roller blinds and anti-glare roller sunscreens for the global marine industry as a result of their seagoing experiences 2 decades earlier.

> *For retailers it's footfall. For factories it's infrastructure. For training Organisations it's car parks / public transport. Every business has its own list of influencing priorities that need to be considered when choosing a site to locate to.*
>
> *There can be a huge band of variance between the priorities of different business types. Business owners must ensure that they think through their future strategy and produce a 5-year plan for their business. If you know where you expect to be in 5 years you will have a much better idea of where you should be now and what type and size of facility you need right now. Relocating is expensive and disruptive. Take your time; make sure you get it right!*

007 - Location, Location, Location

There are television programmes about it but unfortunately they are not really relevant to someone looking to start up a business or relocate an organisation, unless it is involved with buying domestic property.

For most businesses a more profitable bottom line is usually the objective, whereas for a non-profit making organisation it may be the desire to serve as many clients as possible as easily as possible for them, but consequently at a relatively higher cost.

What is important depends on the type of organisation. If you are in retail then it will be passing trade; footfall if you are located in a pedestrian shopping area or car parking and road network if you are out in the sticks on a retail park.

Factories tend to want affordable rent and rates but with good road network, facilities for staff and if they are 'Just in Time' suppliers, the nearer to the major customer the better.

With service providers, it depends if you always go out visiting – if so, location doesn't matter so much, you can maybe even work from home.

Organisations offering training will often have the unemployed as students, so need to be near public transport but also with ample car parking for busy executives who can find some time to train but tend to arrive in a hurry and leave the same way.

Think carefully about the ideal location for your organisation. Consider everything, take your time and make sure you don't opt for just anywhere, simply because it was the first or only option available at the time. The chances are you will have to make a commitment to stay there for a few years, so you need to be sure it is right.

Property leases are notoriously difficult to get out of once entered into, without substantial penalties. It may be better to temporarily set up somewhere that is not ideal but on short term rental agreements, keeping your options open, until the right place presents itself.

Believe me, it is extremely unlikely that the **first** place you look at is going to be the right place or the best option you will find. Do not jump at it because usually there is something better not far behind. It can be difficult if finding somewhere suitable is holding up the project but where 10 year leases, or longer are concerned, you must consider the consequences.

A word of warning for those who are not 'legal savvy'. It is my understanding that in the UK, whilst you probably do need to use a solicitor to finalise the legal part of a lease and do the searches for you, if they get the results of the searches wrong they are not liable for any comeback. Silly, but true. It's a scandal really but if you have to be absolutely sure that something associated with the property is not going to happen in the future, that will or could have a disastrous effect on your business, you cannot leave it to chance, you must carry out your own research as a back-up.

Most probably any research you do will be more effective.

The message is simple. Do your homework carefully and only make a full relocation commitment when you are sure you have found the right property in the right area.

Personally I did work from home for a year or so in the early days. It was a useful and beneficial exercise at the time and helped me to meet my objectives.

For mums with kids the overwhelming advantage of being able to look after their children and still hold down a job that is flexible enough to fit in with the hours and timelines that they can give, is probably all they will consider and they will readily accept any disadvantages.

For everyone else who is able to travel to work, the advantages and disadvantages need to be very carefully weighed up, one against the other before making a decision.

008 - Working From Home

Whilst many employees could probably do their work from home it's odd that most of us don't ever consider it. Possibly because we assume our employer insists or expects, that we will attend our place of work as agreed when we started working for them, whenever that was.

It may be that the employers have never considered asking staff to work from home, thinking that they would be more difficult to monitor and control. In many cases of course it is just not practical. Hospital workers, firemen, bus drivers, dockers and thousands of other jobs need to be carried out at a specific location.

However, certain levels of the people who administer the previously mentioned jobs probably could work from home. With today's advances in communication technology, a hospital telephonist who only works on a switchboard can be located at home and could also be disabled. In fact that would probably apply to many large organisations.

Over the years, as organisations have addressed their overheads and looked at how and where they can save money to become more efficient, some of them have opened up to home working for selected job roles as a cost-cutting exercise. After all if they can close an office or work area, they will save on air conditioning costs and lighting. They don't have to provide canteen or restroom facilities, car parking spaces and if they can shut down the office or other space, they save the rent as well.

With today's technology that includes networked computers, scanners and printers; mobile phones that sing and dance; Video Conferencing via Skype and other providers; it's not surprising that some employers are going for it in a big way.

One problem for the home worker is that they are faced with extra bills for power and lighting as a result of being at home all day, unless their employer reimburses them, which probably defeats one of the advantages for the employer.

By far the biggest number of home workers come under the banner of 'self employed' and this is probably where we are the most concerned. Are winning enterprises located at home? Well a few notable ones have been but they didn't stay there very long because you generally need to employ people to make your business into a winner. Working from home is not really conducive to having a lot of employees working from there as well. Although if you employ a team of people who can work from their own homes it can be successful.

When I worked from home I used to claim back a portion of the household rates, telephone, power and lighting for my study where I worked and whilst my accountant was prepared to do it, it seemed to me to be a bit messy, even though they were genuine claims. I am sure there are tens of thousands of self-employed and employed people who do claim back the additional expenses as legitimate overheads and have no problems.

Just like the working mothers, working from home can be a boon for people with disabilities and they will accept the associated shortcomings, which for me included:

No personal contact with work colleagues, distractions from front door callers and other family members, isolation and generally just not getting out of the house, going to work and meeting people in the flesh.

Is town centre retailing for you or would secondary centres be better? Up to the end of the last century, a high street shop was considered to be the ideal location for most retail outlets. It was usually only the rental price that put shop owners off. Since the advent of electronic retailing on the Internet via the world wide web, many high streets are seeing a decline and in some towns a dramatic deterioration in the number of active, busy, profitable shops.

What was once considered to be the utopia in locating most retail outlets is now very questionable and must be carefully thought through.

009 - Town Centre Retailing

For the first 18 years of my business life, I operated and traded out of shops in Sunderland town centre in North East England and for most of that time I served good old 'Joe Public'.

Any retailer open to the public will have lots of stories to tell about how difficult, dangerous, infuriating, ignorant and just plain thick, some people can be. It goes with the territory and once again I repeat that if it was easy everyone would be doing it, so the more difficult something is to achieve, the greater the rewards can be. Remember that when you are pricing your products. If there is little or no competition you should be applying the 'supply and demand' rule and adding a bit on to compensate you for all of the extra hard work and frustration.

Although the shop was centrally located it did not by any means guarantee me a steady flow of willing customers keen to buy the goods I had to offer. Over the 18 years, I had shops in 2 locations just off the high street where footfall was not as high as the main street and consequently it was sometimes hours between people coming in. When they did arrive we had to apply our very best selling skills but without putting on too much pressure.

We sold and installed (for an extra fee) window blinds and the products and service had to be good. We could take nothing for granted. The only advantage was the rents were not as high as the main high street retailers were paying.

We needed to adopt secondary methods of persuasion to get more prospects into the shop, which are touched on in chapter 22 *'Selling and Sales Techniques',* in this book, with 40 of them being discussed in detail in Book No.2 of this 'Ways 2 Win' series.

I have to admit that for me the high street shop was probably the only way I would have dared start up the kind of business that I did. It made selling, which I found quite difficult at the time, much easier to do, so that I became to enjoy it because I knew I was making people's lives better by supplying them with what they wanted and generally they were complimentary about it.

We used the window display to best advantage and gave the company a name that described what we did. It was called Northern Window Blind Co. so that when we told anyone the name of the company, they did not need to follow it up by asking what we did.

There were a few problems associated with the shop location, of which parking was one (it was often difficult to find a spot near the shop after I had been out on a measure or installation) and it was quite expensive as well. As well as the rent, the rates were also much higher than a factory would have been.

If you are considering a town centre retail shop, or indeed a shop or factory in any location, talk to someone with some knowledge or experience. For example at the end of the lease on our first shop I was gob smacked when I was hit with a *Schedule of Dilapidations* for thousands of pounds that I was not expecting.

Whilst I was a bit more savvy about avoiding a Full Repairing lease with the second shop, managing to get just an internal repairing lease instead, which still cost me a few thousand pounds for the dilapidations, I had signed up for 14 years but left after 12 years and had to pay the other 2 years rent anyway.

Be warned, high street shops can work but Be Careful!!

This is the first shop from where John and Lilian Lightfoot began trading as Northern Window Blind Company, the name they originally chose for today's business. It was located at 2 Bridge Street, SUNDERLAND, and opened on 10th November 1975. John has always believed that a business name and shop window should signify what the business is all about as can be seen in these two photographs.

In January 1983 they moved to a new shop 250 mts away at 204 High Street West. On 27th May 1988 they changed the status of the company from a partnership to a Private Limited Company and called it Solar Solve Ltd, trading as Solar Solve Marine International, one year after introducing the anti-glare roller sunscreens to the marine industry. They traded from this location for almost 10 years before moving the business to a factory unit in their home town of South Shields.

> *Organising yourself will be a vital requirement for the winning entrepreneur. The only alternatives that I can think of if you are not an organised person are to hire someone as a Personal Assistant who is well organised and has your respect and encouragement to organise you; or failure to make the grade and create a winning organisation. I don't think there is anything else in between.*
> *Traits are distinguishing features of your personal nature and throughout this book you will identify that you need to have a whole lot of them including Application, Discipline, Communication and Organisation, which we discuss here.*

010 - Organise Yourself

With all of the other traits that go hand–in–hand with your need to have organisational skills, you won't get far on the Ways 2 Win path without being very well organised.

Work hard at it and prioritise what you NEED to achieve in the short and medium term and not what you WANT to achieve. Most of us arrive at work in the morning with a head full of ideas about what we want and hope to get done that day. Then as the day goes on emails start arriving, or work colleagues need something, or customers are making demands that you didn't expect and before you know it you have a list of jobs that should really be done first because they NEED to be done ASAP - As Soon As Possible. Consequently, very few of the jobs you WANTED to get done are actually completed.

The same thing happens the next day and every day of the week. You must get a system in place that will prioritise all of the work that comes in to you, together with the work you have identified as being a requirement.

The problems associated with the workload are not insurmountable and various options will exist to deal with them. Each job, task, work related requirement that is directed at you, either by you personally or by other people needs to be quickly assessed.

First of all it needs to be established if the work is necessary and if it is, the timescale in which is has to be accomplished. Is it Immediate, Short Term, Medium Term or Long Term (and what the time scales attached to each of these periods actually are)?

The next step is to assess if the task can be competently delegated to someone else and if so be sure that the person doing the work is absolutely clear about what is required of them and what the deadline is – Do Not Assume Anything. Delegating the task does not mean that you have delegated the responsibility as well. Check its progress until it has been satisfactorily completed.

This process should be continuously repeated throughout a busy day, to enable you only to do the other work that needs to be done and never to enable you to do the jobs you WANT to do.

When the nice jobs are eventually accepted as being necessary to improve the organisation, they will have to be prioritised into the 'NEED to be done' slots. Any nice jobs that were more of a fancy than something positive, will fall by the wayside by default and little or no time will have been wasted on them.

Organising your daily schedule should really begin by ensuring that you are always in at work at least 5 minutes before your official start time; ensuring that all of the other employees are in 'On Time' as well. Everyone should understand that 'On Time' means at least 5 minutes before official starting times.

Make sure reference notes for any meetings you attend are completed the day before the meeting, in case you get hit with customer related issues on the day of the meeting when you had hoped to do the notes.

This actually applies to anything and everything you plan to do on any particular day – complete any preparation notes, sales aids, forms, absolutely anything at all, the day before or even sooner if possible.

With this process of organising yourself, you are going to ensure that you become a very well organised winner.

One of the best ways for you and your team to become well organised is to include 'Deadlines' with all decisions regarding time related work. If something is to be achieved during the day, then state by what time that day. If it is required next month give a deadline date or if it is not too critical, a week number may be OK.

It should go without saying that you will need a diary of some sort, with all of your meetings and appointments listed, along with a note of anything that is going to happen on a particular day. For example if you are at a meeting and you agree to ring someone next Wednesday, don't wait for the minutes of the meeting to land on your desk as a reminder – you should put an appropriate note in your diary there and then.

As the person leading a winning organisation you should have a 3-year plan that records the significant occasions you expect to take place in any year. There may be staff reviews, staff meetings, training, seasonal changes to product ranges, a rent review and so on. All of these need to be logged or displayed somewhere, so that other colleagues are aware of them and they also need to be in your diary, with reminders entered 1 or 2 weeks before, so you have plenty of time to prepare for them and where necessary indicate what actions will need to be taken.

Immediate access to well organised filing systems either in paper documents or electronic form will save lots of time and frustration. Creating systems that others can access equally as fast, is the way of a winning business and must be encouraged.

Being well organised is simply common sense. As you work through a typical day think about what is not quite right and if you are being a bit disorganised. If something could be done better next time make a note to address the issue. Keep an eye on your employees also and make suggestions to them about correcting any disorganised practices you have observed.

Once you are organised and running a well organised establishment it comes naturally as time goes on, without even thinking about it.

When it comes to suppliers, owners of very small General Dealers may be able to call into their nearest Cash and Carry depot, fill up their estate car with goods and head back to the shop to restock the shelves and that'll be it – job done.

Self employed Plumbers and Electricians probably won't have it quite so easy, needing to also visit the relevant trade counter of their local merchants for more specialist items.

For many other businesses there will be a need to purchase a variety of goods and services that cannot be bought locally or in some cases have to be imported.

Whatever type of organisation you are associated with it will make good sense to spread the risk and use one or more suppliers for every product you stock, component you buy in or service you require.

011 - Supplier Network

Even if they fall into the first category mentioned above and are able to get all of the supplies needed from one local wholesaler most owners/managers will visit other wholesalers in the area to check on their range of goods, their quality and prices. If they don't then they are not doing their job properly and that applies to all owners/managers of every type of organisation that buys in goods or services, especially the winning enterprises.

Firstly you need to set up a supplier network by finding 3 or 4 alternative suppliers for everything you purchase and then checking them all out to see who offers the best products, service and price. In my manufacturing business' of top brand products at fairly expensive prices, that is our order of priority. The products, components, service all need to be the best, even if we have to pay extra for them, so price is not the major factor.

We pride ourselves on supplying Exactly What our customers want, Exactly When they want it and Exactly Where they want it and to achieve that we need the unwavering support of our suppliers, who like us, charge for that type of service.

If you are involved with market stalls or discount shops then price will no doubt be the major driving factor. Your customers will not expect top quality products for 50 pence apiece and so you will have your own priorities and should set up your supplier network accordingly. All I urge you to do is look around and do not go for the first supplier that has what you are looking for. Take your time to try and find others as you may get a better deal from them.

When I refer to purchases I also include, services like accountancy, payroll, banking, legal, power, ICT (Information and Communication Technology) hardware and software, car maintenance, general maintenance, logistics, plus others.

All of these suppliers operate in a free trade area, in competition with others and will surely want you business, even the bank managers will – so for the ones that come up to your standards, whatever they may be, negotiate with them to see who will be on your Main Suppliers list and which ones will be relegated to the Secondary Suppliers list.

There will be times when, for whatever reason, your Main Supplier cannot fulfil an order for you in the required timescale and that is why you need Secondary Suppliers. The problem though, is that you need to keep Secondary Suppliers and Service Providers happy to work for you at a moments notice but only occasionally. They are unlikely to give you an excellent service if called upon maybe just once or twice a year, if that.

The usual tactic is to give them an occasional order they can quite adequately handle and provide you with a good service, even though it is at a higher price than you would normally pay. A winning organisation would accept this occasional extra cost to ensure it has an effective and efficient back-up strategy in place.

Finally in a winning organisation all of the information relating to Main and Secondary Suppliers and Service Providers will be well documented, kept up to date and discussed with your team on a regular basis. Your Suppliers should be monitored annually, when they advise of price increases usually, to check that they are still giving you the best deal for your needs.

> *In business you can usually make more money by increasing your prices in line with the amount of 'Value' you add to the things you buy, before you sell them on.*
> *At Solar Solve, because we manufacture, supply and install we get lots of opportunities to add value to the products we sell and can therefore increase the resale prices accordingly.*
> *Owners of corner sweet shops on the other hand are going to be pretty limited, as they usually buy a big jar of sweets to sell in small packs and the price of the packets is displayed on the front of the jar. It makes raising the price as a reward for some form of added value rather difficult.*

012 - Adding Value via Production or Service

As well as the examples mentioned above there are many, many more in reality because most enterprises exist to supply goods or services that they have added value to.

An accountant will supply you with some sheets of paper that are stapled together forming a hard copy of your accounts and maybe an electronic set by email or on a USB. Total cost of the paper and stick may be £2 or £3 but you are prepared to pay him around £1,000 for them because he has added information that is useful to your organisation. These days accountants offer all sorts of other services to their clients. They want to add more value to the information they are supplying to you, so they can charge you even more. There might be ways you could add more value.

In my company we ask the customer for only minimum information that is easy for them to acquire and we do all of the preparation work and calculations to come up with the dimensions and other specifications for what they need. We try to make it easy for them and difficult for us because we want them to feel that our higher prices are worth the extra money.

Then we manufacture and dispatch very quickly, faster than our competitors can and use only the best components that are assembled by highly skilled people who care. So even more extra value is added.

The products are all Individually tested and signed off before being packed in sturdy wooden custom made packing cases. They are Type Approved by 3 of the world's foremost Classification Societies and guaranteed to last for a specified number of years depending on the product type. Each packing case of products contains an assortment of useful documents including technical details, installation instructions, packing lists, Customer Questionnaire and a copy of the Chairman's Personal Guarantee inviting anyone who is not happy to contact me. I am very proud of the fact that I have had only one call in 15 years. It was from our second biggest customer who had been upset by a member of staff. That was about 7 years ago.

I am not suggesting we never get things wrong but because the offer is there, when something isn't quite right it seems customers prefer to contact one of the team who liased with them initially to get it sorted that way, rather than bother the chairman.

All of these additional services that we add, contribute to a justified increase in price. If we are required to go anywhere in the world to install the products for our customers it opens up another whole set of opportunities to follow similar principles and make some more good money for the company.

Up to now I have used a couple of easy business types to explain the principle of adding value but there are a lot of business people who buy at fixed wholesale prices and sell at fixed retail prices. Whilst it is eminently acceptable for them to discount the retail price I don't remember seeing any businesses proudly displaying the fact that they **add** a percentage to the recommended retail price for providing a better service.

They have to add value in other ways that will motivate customers to buy more. In other words if they can sell more at full retail price, they will earn more and if the higher sales qualify them for a wholesaler discount so much the better. From here it's pretty much common sense for everyone I guess and so I will pick on the corner sweet shop again.

Window displays need to be inviting, with words that attract like GOOD VALUE, GREAT, SUPER, Discover, NEW, EASY, PROVEN, HEALTH (Cough Sweets?), YOU, HAPPY. There will be many others and at first glance some of them may seem to be dubious but spend time thinking about them, what you have to offer and what you are trying to achieve and you will come up with some good ideas.

Avoid the word SALE. Of course it does attract attention and appeals to people but you want to be maximising the price when adding value, not doing it for nothing.

The inside of the shop is just as important and needs a lot of thought because the window display may get prospects inside but then the product displays will have to shout out "Buy me", with you and your sales staff adding extra encouragement.

Take every opportunity to promote changing seasons, festivities and special events. Promote them on your window and in your displays. Don't just stock Easter eggs and hope people will call in to see if you have any – tell everyone who passes the shop that Easter's coming and you have the gifts they need, to keep their family and friends happy.

You could sell chocolate items that you can add a name to with piped icing or name cards produced on a computer. You will certainly need to do some research on the Internet and physically by visiting sweet shops in other towns for ideas and your town to see what is not being done by your competitors.

Adding extra value is all about defining what the 'norm' is for the product or service you supply or intend to supply. What the customer would get and be happy with. Then, realising that a winning business does not want happy customers, it wants delighted customers, you move everything up a notch, or 2 or 3.

Look for ways that enable you to give more in some way and maximise on them for a higher price or by selling more. If it doesn't work, and sometimes you will get it wrong, just keep looking and trying, because that's what winners do.

All enterprises exist to serve customers, clients or other users and most want them to know of their existence and what they have to offer. To achieve that objective they will need to Market and Promote their organisation to the people or other organisations they want to attract; their targets. Marketing, Promotion and Selling are all covered in Book 2 in this Ways 2 Win series because there are so many aspects to it and I doubt if one book will cover them all. In the meantime you need to have understanding of how vital the subject is and the difference between the two.

013 - Promoting Your Organisation

Promotion can be considered as a somewhat less aggressive version of Marketing. It is referred to by Marketing academics as one of the 4 P's; the processes that make up the Marketing function; the others being Product; Place and Price. You will read more about all of them in the first chapter of Book 2. By the use of promotion you will bring to the attention of targets and prospects what it is that you to have offer, so that hopefully they will buy from you. It can be achieved in lots of different ways and will almost certainly consist of a combination of many of them if it is going to be successful.

Promotion via paid-for publicity consists of things like Advertising, Posters, Displays of varying types, Signage and distribution of Fliers.

There are usually many opportunities available to benefit from free or relatively free publicity also. They include Press or News Releases, Newsletters and Sales Presentations as a voluntary speaker to interested groups and organisations. Special offers are a popular way to bring a new product to people's attention and for sports clubs it could be discounted first year fees for example.

You must use any and every opportunity to self-promote whenever you can. Don't decide that you will send out a PR (Press Release) when something good or different happens because it will never happen and lots of promotional opportunities will be lost. Do what my winning company does and decide that you will send out a Press Release or publish your own Press Release every 2 weeks, or week, or month – on a specific date and make sure you do. Find something to tell your targets about that happened in the period since the last one. If nothing happened of significance you have to use your imagination. I am not suggesting you tell lies, just be a bit creative with the truth.

If a supplier is introducing a new line and you take it, do a PR about it. You are now stocking Brand X and so on. It does not matter if all of the other similar businesses in your area are also selling it – they probably won't be bothering to tell anyone; even if it isn't as spectacular as you are making out. At least the name of your business is being brought to everyone's attention.

The difference between Marketing and Promotion is slight. You market your business by stating that you have a shop that sells sweets. You promote it by adding that you have free confectionary demonstrations on Wednesday afternoons.

If you hire someone or promote an employee; put out a PR. Making a donation to a local charity will be appreciated by the community but only if you let people know and have a photo taken handing over the cheque. It has to be organised and co-ordinated but it gets publicity in the run-of-paper, which readers usually pay more attention to, than the pages of adverts or classifieds. I have always found that a PR article printed for free within a newspaper or magazine will be seen by many more people than a paid-for advert in the same publication.

To be a winner you have to be different; think outside of the box, do what others are not doing and not what they are doing. There will be times when you have to do what they are doing as well; so do it better. If you want to just jog along with the others you will be an 'also ran' just like them. Being a winner requires hard work and dedication and never actually switching off. That is not to say you cannot relax and enjoy yourself but always be aware of what is going on around you and if you are genuinely stimulated, the rest will happen naturally and in a pleasant rewarding way that will keep you motivated and happy.

As well as the usual ways to promote your organisation there are many others, depending on what product or service you supply and to whom.

Solar Solve employees know how vital it is to promote the company and are always happy to get involved. It makes a change from the day-to-day routine and does wonders for the business. Every year they have a photo taken that is stuck inside all 400 Christmas cards that are sent out. The photos for 2008 and 2009 are seen above. The company also sends out regular press releases about significant orders but occasionally includes employee training award successes, Solar Solve's Business and Export awards and their Charity donations. These press releases are sent to the local evening newspaper because it is the sort of news that the local community is interested in reading about and encourages owners of other local businesses to get involved by sending in their news. Examples of these events are on the next page.

If you are starting up or running an organisation you should have an objective for its future in your mind. Something that you want to achieve for it, or the products / services that you provide. If you want your products to be the best in the world (and who doesn't?), then you need to write it down and tell the whole world what you are aiming for. If they are not already aware of it then your employees will certainly be interested to know what you are aiming for – as will your customers and goodness only knows who else. Mission and Vision and other Statements are a way of getting your message across!

014 - Mission, Vision and Other Statements

Whilst training for my Institute of Directors Diploma in Company Direction I referred to some of their business books; talked to their course lecturers at Durham University Business School and their examiners at the Pall Mall headquarters in London. If there was one thing I did learn it is that there is much confusion about Mission and Vision Statements. Not about the need for them but more about what each of them should make reference to.

If the IoD cannot get it right, what chance have the rest of us mere mortals got and in any event does it really matter?

As long as the head of an organisation ensures they have a Mission Statement and a Vision Statement, and they do need both, who cares which of the two headings they go under.

To make this article have some kind of logic I will follow what I consider to be the meaning of each one.

An example of a mission statement would be: - "to ensure *40 Ways 2 Win In Business* becomes the best read business book in the whole world".

An example of a Vision Statement would be: - "to build Ways 2 Win books into a multi million pound empire within three years".

The problem is that some would say they should be the other way around. Whatever you might think about it and I suggest you don't spend too much time on the debate, the important factor is to ensure you have both a Mission Statement and a Vision Statement documented for your organisation.

You need to give a lot of thought to where you are trying to place your products and / or services in the market place and then write between 1 and 3 sentences to condense them into achievable objectives. I contend that this will be your Mission Statement.

Then consider where you expect your organisation to be in a certain number of years time, or what impact you expect your products will have on your target markets or the whole world in years to come and give these objectives the same treatment. This will be your Vision Statement.

The Mission Statement and Vision Statement are extremely important. Make them part of your organisation's Aims and Objectives, Reasons for being Established, or Quality Manual if you have one.

But don't leave it there. Ask yourself if you have covered everything with these two statements. Just because it is considered good practice to have two, that does not mean you cannot have more than two.

At Solar Solve we have included a couple of Company Mottos "*Our customers are kings and must be treat like royalty*". And "*Right first time, on time, every time for every customer*".

We also have 4 Basic Values – 1) *'Our people are the source of our strength. They provide the company's corporate intelligence and determine its reputation and vitality'*. 2) *'Involvement and teamwork are our core human values'*. 3) *'Our products are the end result of our efforts, and they will be of the highest quality and reliability. As our products are viewed, so are we viewed'*. 4) *'Profits are the ultimate measure of how efficiently we provide customers with the best products to meet their needs. Profits are essential to grow the company. Growing the company is essential for its long term survival'*.

Finally we have also added Solar Solve's 5 Golden Rules Of Success but I won't bog you down with them, I'm sure you get the message.

Once documented the Mission Statement, Vision Statement and any others need to be prominently displayed for customers and especially employees to see. Most importantly of all, so everyone knows what it is they need to be continually working to retain, or striving towards if you are not yet outright winners.

To my mind this should be the easiest principle of all for winning entrepreneurs and business managers to understand. I can appreciate to some extent that employees may take some persuading, although it is so black and white I have little patience with the non-believers. I see employees who treat customers badly as being plain ignorant. I have no time for them or their negative attitudes and show them the door.

Without customers a business cannot survive, so no matter how difficult they may be, you have to embrace them and give them what they want. If you don't, they will find a competitor who will. Like it or not.. The Customer Is King!!

015 - Your Customer Is King / Queen

Just about every organisation needs customers of one kind or another, which means the employees rely on customers for their living. I cannot understand why there are still so many businesses around that consider their customers to be nuisances, distractions and generally just a pain in the neck – or worse.

I see and hear about employees who often seem as if they are going out of their way to make life difficult for the customer, by maybe sighing after being asked a question, or not offering advice or information until it is eventually extracted by the customer asking the right questions. I would like to think these are the exceptions rather than the rules but it could be as high as 50 out of 100 and that is high. With a few exceptions, the 50 that are positive are still not winners. They are mostly good but not great. Pleasant enough, up to a point, as their training demands but not going the extra mile although you might get an extra furlong.

The 5 employees out of the 100 that really treat customers like royalty are the ones who are prepared to do whatever it takes to delight their customers, not just make them happy. If they deal with customers face to face (unless they work in a funeral parlour), they will be bright and happy or similarly disposed, depending on the product or service provided. They should always make eye-contact, be genuine, use words like 'No Problem', 'Absolutely', 'Yes', 'Can Do', 'Is there anything else you need?'

Employees talking to customers by telephone quickly need to establish that they can be heard clearly and understood correctly and that they are also hearing well and understanding everything. It's no use putting the phone down after a 5 minute conversation and wondering to yourself what it was all about. Take your time, talk slowly and clearly, you may have an accent that is difficult for some people to understand but even in your own town many people are still nervous when talking on the telephone, especially with strangers. So take your time and be thorough.

If you offer products or services that some people find somewhat daunting, maybe a motor repair centre, only go into the technicalities if the customer is enquiring that way. Unless you are talking to a fellow expert you should tone down on specifics and maybe just tell them what it does and why they need it – *'The current one is worn out!'* Another point here is I have never had much faith in car repair shops, except the ones that show you the parts that have been replaced and offer to put them in a box in your boot. My other hang-up with them is the bad practice of quoting the basic cost of the parts, then after the job has been done, it is two or three times the quoted price because they didn't include the labour charges or sales tax. There may be some laws against it now but in any event it is a great example of treating customers like dirt, rather than like royalty. I am sure that these days though, such practices have ceased.

You will have just read in the previous chapter that the Solar Solve Company Motto is "*Our customers are kings and must be treat like royalty*". I make no apologies for repeating it. It is probably the maxim on which we put most emphasis. The other customer orientated statement that governs our operations is *"Right first time, on time, every time for every customer"*.

All customers should be treat exactly the same and made to feel as if they are the only customer you have, at the centre of everything you are doing . Remember *'The Reward For Work Well Done Is The Opportunity To Do More'*, which is what a winning enterprise will be achieving every day of the week – not just occasionally.

There is a whole plethora of Red Tape, legislation and other stuff that the modern day business owner/manager has to contend with. Eleven examples are mentioned in the article but the list is in no way exhaustive. They are all required to be complied with by law in one-way or another and can be pretty off-putting. Certainly some, if not all, will cause a degree of mental stress or pain, though not physical.

Unfortunately, as manager of an organisation you have no choice but to take on the pain. Almost certainly you will gain though as a result.

016 - No Pain, No Gain

Red Tape, Government Legislation and Political Correctness can all be a huge source of pain for most organisations, large, medium or small.

Employment Law, Health and Safety, First Aid, Risk Assessment, Fire Wardens, Data Protection Act, Consumer Act, VAT, Customs and Excise, Inland Revenue, PAYE, to name just some. The mind boggles and the list probably puts a lot of budding entrepreneurs right off going beyond the 'thinking about it' stage.

Owners and managers must feel that such directives were sent to haunt them. In fact a lot of what emanates under these 3 banners is common sense and makes for sound business practice and improvement, although there will always be the exceptions of course.

Take the case of political correctness when employing people. A job vacancy arises within a group of eight young women all unskilled and for the sake of political correctness the manager has appointed a 63-year-old man, who is able to do the job, as the ninth team member. He then faces a dilemma because the eight young ladies are unhappy about the appointment.

If you think about it, had a 63-year-old man decided to start a business and employed 8 such females to help him run it, the chances are that they would have accepted such a working relationship scenario and probably they would have made a successful nine-person team.

So why shouldn't it work in the example? Maybe the eight women should not be consulted because then they would be telling the manager to act in a way that he can no longer legally do. The best course of action would be for the manager to meet with the existing employees and explain the new legislation and exactly what it means with regard to how he has to act.

I have experience of a situation where eight young men work quite happily in a factory with an older lady and I am sure that neither the young men nor the lady even think about it as an issue.

The suggestion is simple. Do not dismiss the directives out of hand just because they are new and may sound silly. First reactions are often that they have not been well thought out and sometimes this is the case. However, if they are legislative then they are the law.

So don't always try to analyse a situation (eight young women and one old man) just give it a try, it may work for you.

A manager at Claridge's Hotel in London was asked why they often take on some very difficult and complicated projects and customers. He implied that if it seemed to be achievable, no matter how difficult that would be and if it would make them money they went for it because his team liked a challenge. They enjoyed being different and all got a real sense of satisfaction when it came to fruition and they had lots of delighted customers.

His parting comments though were probably the most telling and realistic, when he implied that if they discussed a challenge too much and thought too deeply about it they would find plenty of reasons why they should not do it. Yet every time they take on such challenges they are successful and usually make money.

The moral is that you can take the easy route, stay as you are, stick firmly and solidly with what you know and continue to jog along quite happily as an 'also-ran'. Or you can go the route of Claridge's and many other winners, including Solar Solve and take on the jobs that your competitors either cannot do, or more to the point, cannot be bothered to do.

At Solar Solve we were just ordinary window blind makers and suppliers working from a high street shop, mainly supplying Joe Public who was not very demanding and tended to accept whatever was being offered as adequate, which it actually was, for use inside domestic homes.

Then we were asked to quote for roller sunscreens for ships that had to be made up from special solar films that are not manufactured in the UK. They had to be housed in aluminium cassettes that were going to have to be imported. There needed to be documentary evidence regarding the materials used in the manufacture of all components including the flame retardant roller blind fabrics and blackout materials.

All of the products we supply have to be manufactured to Quality Assured Standards that some customers ask to see. We have them Type Approved for use in Marine Environments by not one but three classification societies... and there is more, much more. I could write a whole book about all of the pain a specialist roller blind manufacturer has to endure getting it all right.

With all of these additional hoops to jump through, it's not surprising that out of around 1,000 roller blind manufacturers in the UK, there is only one that specialises in Roller Blinds and Roller Sunscreens for the Marine Industry globally. Even though, when done properly, any business can gain from pain and reap substantial rewards as a winning enterprise.

"No pain – No gain" is a statement about life itself, as is "The Risk equals The Reward". Budding entrepreneurs who want to avoid being employees all of their lives have to realise this and take up the challenge. It's unlikely to come to you. You have to go out and find it. Tens of thousands of people do and never regret it.

First Impressions Count – An old fashioned saying maybe but one that has stood the test of time and is just as true today as it has always been.

From personal appearance, tidiness and cleanliness of workplace to presentation of product or service and beyond YOU WILL GET ONLY ONE CHANCE TO MAKE A FIRST IMPRESSION SO MAKE IT COUNT – BIG TIME.

As a business owner / manager, not only you but everything around you to do with your business has an influence on how you are perceived by your customers and prospects and indeed all of your stakeholders.

017 - First Impressions Count

Personal appearance is usually considered to be most important and smart dress is almost always readily acceptable as the 'norm' for anyone wanting to create a good first impression with whomever it is that they are meeting.

Often some type of uniform may be adopted, which indicates an inherent discipline that is favoured by many. This can be a real asset providing everyone wears the uniform and they are maintained clean and smart.

If you make presentations they must be well rehearsed and given in a polished, confident manner with equipment and aids in good working order. In view of today's sometimes temperamental technology it could be wiser not to use hi-tech equipment if it is not necessary. I have been a delegate at many presentations that were totally devastated due to malfunctioning technical gear.

Your workplace, be it retail shop, factory, office or whatever else must be clean, tidy and orderly, indicating exactly those qualities to the people whom you wish to impress.

The product you sell, whether it is an item, document or even entertainment, must be well made and may need to be well packaged 'to appeal'. If it has to be packaged for delivery this is another great opportunity to create a good impression with your customer. Think about the very best way it can be packed to make their life easier and then delight them by doing it.

If you sell a service make sure you do it well. Verify with your customer exactly what you are going to do and why. If you make a mess, tidy up after you.

Never, ever let the phone ring more than 3 times. To impress the caller, who could be a potential customer, it should be answered during the first ring tone, every time as a matter of course and not just as a stroke of luck. If that is difficult then you need to employ more people to answer the phone or train every employee to answer the phone and take messages, depending on the type of organisation you run. A human being who answers politely, offers to take a message and guarantees the caller will be rung back is better than a long wait or an answering machine.

Smile and be friendly towards your customers and give them your undivided attention, do not be distracted by anyone or anything; not only is it the height of bad manners it is very off-putting for them. Next time they may go to a smiling, friendly and attentive competitor.

Whatever it is that is great about your organisation; whether it is you, your staff, your workplace, your sales aids, your reliability, your product or service, make sure it is relayed to your customer in order to impress them.

If, after supplying your product to a customer they come back to you with a problem, you have no option but to move heaven and earth to take advantage of what will probably be your last chance to make a good first impression.

The message is simple – Throughout every stage of the many procedures you use to win an order and supply your product, a new opportunity arises to create a good first impression.

Make sure you take every opportunity and always get them right. Hopefully orders will follow.

The photo above was taken after the Solar Solve team had undertaken a training course in the use of fire extinguishers. They had been told not to wear their uniform clothes. Do the names Rag, Tag and Bobtail spring to mind?

The photo below, of the same people, shows them in uniform. At Solar Solve we feel that the wearing of uniforms gives a much better impression of both the individual and the organisation they work for. I hope you agree.

The photo above was taken by the captain of 'The World' the largest privately owned residential yacht on the planet, who was so impressed with the quality of the solar screens and the Solar Solve team he offered to take the photo as a memento and so that it could be used in a press release about the job.

Sometimes the Solar Solve marketing team will include a photo of the people who work for the business on their sales aids, so that customers and prospects can put the face to a name when communicating with the company, to make it more personal.

The Magnificent Solar Solve *Marine* Team

If The Sun Is A Problem - We can *SOLA*SOLV It

Shading The World From The Port of Tyne, South Shields, UK

Paul H; Jamie; Julie; Adam S; Krys; Adam R; Ian R; Ian S; Lilian; Ron; Sheila; Mal; Leanne; Mark; Avis; John; Paul M; Carl

Gone are the days when an owner manager could set his or her sights on the exact type of person they wanted to fill a particular role within their organisation. Interviewing people until the ideal candidate (in your opinion) presented himself or herself and was hired to the exclusion of and without due regard to all others, has been banished to the history books. Personal opinions about current employment law should play no part in today's procedures for selecting new employees. The law is the law and you must abide by it!

018 - Getting The Right People

Business managers the world over, if they are honest, will all agree –there is no such person as the perfect employee – except for themselves, of course.

If they are carrying out their Human Resources responsibilities properly they will have a job description, relevant application form (not a general one for all types of employee) and unfortunately a picture in their mind of just exactly the right type of person they are looking for. Someone ideal who will be perfect for the job and who will help to take the organisation forward in leaps and bounds.

As soon as the returned Job Applications start coming in, reality begins to dawn. Out of 60 responses surely there must be 6 people who can be invited in for first interviews? Well 4 then?
Maybe we should look again at the advert and the Job Description. Re-advertise, advising previous applicants not to re-apply and start all over again.

Of course now that we are politically correct and conforming to all of the appropriate legislations we have a totally open mind. Although the job is to work with a group of 8 young women all unskilled and all aged between 25 and 30 you have given equal consideration to everyone. From the skills and ability viewpoint there is a 63-year-old man who could do the job but the 8 women are not happy. Where do you go from there?

Using your best guess you select a few people for interview believing what they have written. A check with their previous employer who is so scared that they will be taken to court if they say anything negative, informs you the person was fine whilst working for them.

For the interview it is necessary to do all of the right preparation and ask searching, informative questions. Again, you have to believe what you are told even though we all know there is a tendency for most people to oversell themselves at job interviews. You should also run some written tests. There are organisations that are in business to go through the whole process for you and will insist they are very good at it.

About the only successful way to get the right person is to employ them and to review their progress after 3, 6, and 9 months – pointing out any problems and working towards resolving them. During this period, if it is obvious that you have made the wrong choice, then you have a chance to rectify it.

In my 40 odd years of employing people I learned a very long time ago that the person with the most qualifications to do a job is not usually the best person for the job. In certain jobs of course people must hold qualifications but in that case the most highly qualified applicant is unlikely to be the best person for you.

I look for people with the right attitude, who are prepared to commit to the job and the organisation employing them. If the person is right and they love coming into work, you can usually train them to do the job they were hired for and indeed to multi-skill them for many other work related tasks as well.

You must reciprocate by treating your employees well and with respect. You will only know for sure if you have picked the right person once they are "on board" and you make it your business to monitor and help them to succeed from the word "go".

Getting the right people is not easy but if you succeed your organisation will certainly benefit.

> *Most business owners/managers deliberate for a long time before taking on their first employee. Usually because they feel there is not enough work to keep someone gainfully employed full time – they only need Half a Person. A part time employee is an option they don't really want to consider. Does it mean they have to employ someone full time and run the organisation at a loss until they find enough work to keep them busy all the time? How long does that usually take? Can they afford to stand the loss? Can they afford not to?*

019 - Half A Person

For the one-person organisation the time will come when more help is needed and for whatever reason, part time workers are not the answer. Maybe they are a possibility but would hiring one be the right decision, bearing in mind that you hope to need more help in the future and can not easily dismiss a dedicated part time employee in favour of a full time one at a later stage?

It really can be a minefield and very often results in no decision at all, the principal continuing to plod along alone, over-worked and frustrated. Ring any bells? Well many of us have already been there, so a few pointers may help.

Firstly, be sure you need more help. Could you not reorganise yourself better and become more efficient at what you do, so generating more output in the same time?

Could you outsource some of your work? Would it be more cost effective?

Business managers who did opt to take the plunge and employ someone full time, even though they probably thought they could not keep them fully employed, usually report that they had new employees fully occupied within weeks of taking them on.

Initially it is a case of Parkinson's Law; "Work expands so as to fill the time available for its completion ".

Gradually though, usually because the owner/manager has been freed up to concentrate on running and directing the business as well as looking for more orders, the extra hours that were perceived to be 'free', become filled with useful work and the business starts to grow.

As long as managers realise that the extra help is in place to allow them to concentrate on generating more business and not so that they can be distracted into doing anything else, particularly going off to play golf or whatever, then there is every chance that they will succeed. Going off site to do some business networking, if it results in more sales, is OK even if it does entail having to play a round of golf. Becoming a winner is all about having a 'whatever it takes' attitude.

After a while, more income will be the order of the day and with the extra effort put in to succeed, it will not be long before the new person has no time to waste. Multi tasking is a great way to make this happen sooner rather than later and so a new employee who is flexible about learning and applying additional skills would be an asset.

When it comes to needing a second and then subsequent employees, the decision is never as difficult as the first time round.

My advice would normally be to establish for certain that you do need extra help. Then ask yourself "If I did employ someone what would be the chances of my being able to look for and win some additional work?"

If the answer is "fair, good or excellent" then go for it because that is nearly always the right decision.

Whilst there are many successful one-person businesses out there, some of which may already be winners, their chances of making a lot of money usually increase significantly if they employ people to help them make the business grow and become a generator of bigger profits.

Delegation is definitely a skill and often referred to as an art. You will have heard the term 'The Art of Delegation'. The biggest hurdle for managers is finding people whom they can trust enough to do their work and get it right – every time. Then there is the requirement for patience whilst the tasks are being taught and the need for discipline to hold back from jumping in to do it yourself, at the very teeniest of signs that things are going slightly off course. Delegation takes time but is well worth the commitment.

020 - Delegation

In some books directed at the business manager the subject of delegation is often referred to as the "art" of delegation. Seen by many as one of the biggest obstacles to their progress, the main problem is getting past the barrier of *"it's usually quicker and easier to do it myself".*

Could a General who was a master swordsman win a battle without trusting his soldiers to fight to their best ability? If he wanted to do all of the fighting himself just because he was the best at it, he would soon be overwhelmed.

You may feel that you have lots of able workers and think that the problem lies with the managers. Well, the General needs his lieutenant's just as much as he needs his soldiers, he can't do all of their work either; he must delegate and trust them, too.

If you feel that you have "inherited" staff you consider to be incapable, incompetent or both, you could have a genuine problem and must address the situation somehow. Before doing anything however, you need to analyse yourself. Make sure the problem does not lie with you.

Are you a good communicator?
Are your people properly and fully trained?
Are they capable of doing the job?
Are they willing to take the responsibility?
Are procedures and processes in place for the tasks you need to delegate?

Self analysis is not easy and unless you have a good working relationship with some of your colleagues who will tell you honestly what they think, it could be a difficult task. But you must make every endeavour to get yourself sorted before moving on to consider your employees.

It doesn't have to be an art; delegation is just simple common sense with a good deal of trust.

Think Richard Branson. Think Virgin Organisation and you have to Think *Delegation*. There is no way he could have established such a highly successful organisation with its hugely differing business types without delegating. My impression is that Richard Branson has the vision, drive, enthusiasm and determination and delegates everything else. Similarly of course with just about every highly successful multi-billionaire entrepreneur.

The skill is finding the right people to put in place and then delegate to them all of the tasks they can do well. Finding the right people to work for you is a whole other topic all of its own and is covered in Chapter 18. In the meantime give some serious thought to which of your current work responsibilities you could quite easily delegate to someone else with a little bit of your time and some simple training to get them qualified and signed-off as capable.

Delegation is one of the most difficult objectives to get employees to put into effect and yet a few months after 'letting go' they usually not only forget they used to do the task, they do not miss doing it, because often they have moved on and are doing more demanding, challenging work that has been delegated to them, and enjoying it more. For business owners that could mean more customer contact or marketing of your company.

Once the easier tasks have been delegated successfully you should move on to transferring some of the more difficult tasks. Not only will you have more time to concentrate on leading and directing the business or your part of it but another great benefit is that there should be no noticeable effect on how it operates when you are on holiday or off site for any reason.

If conversations are not recorded in some way, verbal communication can be a nightmare when it causes confusion that then results in serious consequences. Without a record, audio or visual, there is no facility to assign blame, which unfortunately may end up as a requirement if there needs to be an investigation. Written or documented communication is always best and you should ensure that it happens for mutual clarification and to safeguard your position. Good communication is the essence of a great organisation!

021 - Communication

As a business manager you may suffer from suppliers who can't get your delivery requirements right or the quantity ordered correct. They may get the description of the goods wrong or over charge a verbally agreed price.

Then there are your employees who cannot seem to follow even the simplest of instructions and don't appear to have a clue about what is going on in your organisation even though you have told them a million times before. Well, lots of times anyway.

And of course the customers just don't seem to know exactly what it is they want. You supply what they ordered but all they do is complain about the price agreed, the quantity requested and the fact it's not what they asked for anyway. If it was all done verbally, without a written follow-up to review the order details, which needs to be signed or confirmed in some other way by the customer, then who got what wrong? Who is to blame?

If this sounds like something you have experienced, the problem could be poor communication.

When ordering from suppliers, don't rely on them to guess at what you require from vague information. Unless an order is clear and concise in every way and is written down, there is a great possibility that it will be wrong. If you must place an order quickly by phone or verbally in some other way, either follow it up in written format by email / fax or have the supplier confirm it to you in writing, before despatch.

The opposite will be required if you are the supplier – always confirm exactly what you are going to supply, how many, when and at what price, in writing and ask for your customer's confirmation. It is referred to as a "Contract Review" and can save a lot of hassle later and substantial amounts of money, especially if initial orders are contracted verbally. Whilst it is my experience that this method is not absolutely foolproof, it can be much more effective than verbal-only contracts. It works for my company 99% of the time. I have found nothing that is perfect (because our customers are always right!) or better, that causes minimal hassle for the customer, who very often cannot understand why such procedures are necessary – but they definitely are.

Managers who are good, effective communicators have few problems with their staff. Again, always be clear and concise about what you want. If it is possible to use Work Request dockets, they can be of immense value, indicating who raised it, what is required, by when and who is requested to carry out the task. A space for completion by the employee indicating that the job has been done, when it was completed, parts used, other remarks etc is also useful. To some extent the dockets are being replaced by emails and company Intranets but I personally still like the bits of paper that sit on a persons desk until the job is done and it has been returned. Cyberspace must be congested with the billions of electronic job sheets that 'went missing'.

Once again it is a case of eliminating misunderstandings over verbal communication.

Finally, keeping all employees aware of what is going on is definitely an art form and often the most contentious issue of all. Just like Health and Safety issues it is not enough to post information on notice boards in staff rooms. You have to bring it to every individual's attention. The most effective way of doing this, though not always foolproof, is to include initial boxes on the document. At least it helps to keep you in the clear. If the information is of vital importance you may need a follow up with a question and answer discussion. Once again a lot of time and effort for the overworked business manager but good communication is vital for a winning organisation.

To have a winning enterprise you will almost certainly need to sell something, either personally or via some means that you have set up for the purpose. Concern about the ability or rather the inability to sell is one of the major factors that put people off becoming self-employed. But just like most of the other objections, it can be overcome if tackled in the right way. I always thought that there was a lot of truth in the statement that 'good salesmen are born and not bred' and it worried me at first. However, whilst I still believe there are 'natural born salesmen and women' I now know that anyone who is committed to the cause can be trained to become a good salesperson; with some of them going on to become great salespeople.

022 - Selling and Sales Techniques

Probably the first thing you should take to heart in the Intro-Box is that if you are not confident at selling then hire someone who is. Do not let it put you off creating a winning organisation – I didn't and it has worked fine for me.

If, like me, you want to learn some selling skills to see how you get on, then there will be other books available in this *Ways 2 Win* series, that cover marketing of your business and selling skills. I include clever marketing as part of selling and it will take at least one separate book, possibly up to 3 to cover the many aspects of selling and sales techniques. However, nobody is likely to need to know all of them because they vary widely depending on a business's products and services offered.

As a manufacturing exporter I need to be travelling the world and concentrating on a global market, whereas someone selling Olde Fashioned Candies from a stall in a shopping mall may not have to look any further that the pedestrians walking by the stall.

I emphasise that I NEED to work globally; but my displays in the factory do not have to be really, really eye-catching because my customers never visit us. We take some samples with us but our product is not so much about aesthetics as functionality and we source our targets and prospects using marketing techniques.

The candy seller needs to have an impressive display that stops people from walking by without looking and maybe some kind of offer to tempt them into buying. Whilst they are buying the sweets on offer and looking round whilst being served, it probably won't take much of a chat line from a persuasive sales assistant to get them to also purchase something at the full price.

I'm sure everyone knows the candies on special offer are referred to as the 'loss leaders' and most businesses have some form of loss leading product or service. Nothing wrong with that because ultimately it's all about doing whatever it takes to get a sale, as long as it is honest, scrupulous and eventually turns a profit. It will be the case that some customers will not buy more that the special offer product but the term 'Loss leader' is a bit of a misnomer anyway and usually the vendor will make some profit or at least break even.

Where the candy seller may be able to expand globally, without having to move from the stall or embark on world-wide sales trips is via the Internet. They already have a stock of goods for sale and a risk taker would be happy to invest some time and money looking at the possibilities and costs of such a venture. In fact the Internet has now opened up some great opportunities for the vast majority of businesses and all other organisations.

Although I do not consider myself to be a good salesman, I think I am excellent at marketing. I get by fine when I am selling because I only sell products I know about and have great faith in. I give the customer the facts and all of the benefits they will get from owning it but then I step back and leave them to decide. There is no pressure – I hate high pressure salespeople.

The reason I enjoy marketing so much is because I am in more of my comfort zone as I am not doing face-to-face selling. I can be very creative about thinking what marketing methods to adopt and how to design the sales aids. Which segment of the market to target and all sorts of other things that are really interesting and inspiring. Read more in my *Ways 2 Win at Marketing* books.

Solar Solve adopt many different sales techniques to sell their products to a global marine market including international exhibitions, often referred to as Trade shows. The photo above was taken at APM 2010, the Asia Pacific Maritime exhibition in Singapore, in March 2010. Julie and I manned the stand although I do try to let other competent (and they do have to be trained and competent) marketing staff members work the exhibitions these days whenever they can. I do like doing the trade shows, even just visiting and they work for us but won't be ideal for everyone to sell from. They will always be worth going to as a visitor though.

Solar Solve also sends out 2 press releases every month to the marine trade journals and local evening paper, who run most of them. (See below).

We all know that some customers are 'unrealistic' or difficult on purpose, as part of their character, to screw down a supplier to get the very best deal that they can. In Business-to-Business, for most Purchasing Officers it is a way of life, part of their Job Description. For lots of ordinary folk it is simply a challenge that they enjoy being part of.

As the owner of a business you must always decide "What is best for the business?" If you are thinking about supplying something 'at cost' or maybe even at a loss you need to be getting something else in return like free advertising or promotion. Or maybe much needed cash to help cash flow and thus avoid a financial disaster.

If not, then what would be the point? You will no doubt be in business to make money so don't let smooth talking customers who may be feeding your ego with compliments or the like, get away with a cheaper price for a product or service that is excellent.

023 - Customer Expectations vs Reality

"As a business owner I do realise how important my customers are", is a statement an average owner or manager would make.

"As a business owner I do know how absolutely vital my customers are to the future of my business", is the statement a winning owner or manger would make. So you can probably guess whose side I am on when it comes to customers' demands.

I am very much customer orientated and suggest to people who often feel that their customers' expectations are somewhat unrealistic; "Maybe you should start to think outside the box".

At Solar Solve the only complaint we ever get and I do mean the ONLY complaint is price. We get price objections at least once every day and as a Brand Leader we come to expect it. In response we patiently explain that quality of product and service comes at a price.

The majority of customers accept it and will pay the price

because they know they will get EXACTLY WHAT they want, EXACTLY WHEN they want it and EXACTLY WHERE in the world they want it. Some of them are happy to pay because they have had bad experiences in the past from cheaper suppliers.

Of course there are those who will just not pay the extra cost, either not knowing or not caring that 'a watch is not just a watch'.

You do not usually find a Rolex watch for sale at a heavily discounted price way below its thousands of dollars price tag and I guess most of us would not expect to, even though, for the most part, it just tells you the time the same as any other watch. In fact some watches priced at less than $100 will not just tell you the time but will throw in your heart rate, altitude, underwater depth and a whole host of other things that the Rolex cannot do.

I know owning a Rolex is also a piece of jewellery as well as a status symbol and is in a league that most of us can only dream of aspiring to. To a much lesser extent I managed to create a significant brand at associated prices by studying and applying the philosophies of some of the world's leading brands like Coca Cola, Ford Motor Company and many others.

It is interesting that both Coca Cola and Ford have made a number of pretty major marketing errors in the past but their Brands were strong enough to overcome the associated fallout.

So in essence, if you are offering the very best quality of product and service at an associated higher price, then your customer is entitled to expect you to jump through hoops to earn the extra money. They may be making unrealistic requests but they are paying you for the privilege, so smile and get on with it.

Usually there are lucrative opportunities for businesses with this attitude and philosophy, because so many businesses out there are just not interested in anything that is difficult or problematic for them. They are always and only, looking for the easy option.

Winners will offer solutions customers want and will pay for.

A winning business owner or manager will always know where any threat of competition is likely to come from. After all, the last thing you want is to suddenly find that you are losing business rapidly when you were not expecting it.
Declining trade is bad enough when you can see it coming, but at least it does give you the opportunity to fight it by creating and implementing alternative plans for survival.
How do you find out if you have any competition and if so, how much of a threat they may be? The following information will be very useful to you as you will be lucky if you don't have any competitor, so be prepared!!

024 - Know Who Your Competitors Are

There will be many external factors affecting your winning enterprise, some of which you will have no control over. They will include situations like recession, extremes of weather, legislation and fashion trends. I trust you have realised that depending on what your organisation does, the above examples could be good or bad for it. For example in a recession a middle market retailer may suffer, whereas a discount shop could benefit. With extremes of weather a ski shop might do well whereas a camping supplier suffers if there are extreme periods of rainstorms.

Try to figure out similar examples for legislation and fashion trends but no prizes I'm afraid.

Competition is usually not-so-good news, tending to have a negative affect on a business, unless a determined manager fights back, which ultimately could benefit the business.

Establishing who and where your competitors are can be easy for some and difficult but not impossible for others.

I mentioned in another chapter that the local corner sweet shop owner only has go round the town occasionally to check up on his competitors, to see if they have come up with any new ideas or related products that could be a threat; or to see if any new sweet shops have opened or existing ones closed.

Some other business types like builders merchants will probably hear if anyone has opened up in competition either by word-of-mouth through customers or advertising that has been placed by the competition.

For just about all types of organisations the Internet on the World Wide Web will offer something useful. It may be the chance to sell your products electronically to the whole world or maybe even just to advertise your products to your target market.

The Internet is one really useful place you can go to check out the competition. If you are an accountant located in Timbuktu you simply log onto the Internet and type in *accountants located in Timbuktu* and if you have any competitors they will be listed there for you. Possibly not all of them but 90% of them will be.

The next step then is to research each one to assess how much of a threat any of them might be. Depending on what you do, some of them may not be. If you are an accountant that specialises in payroll and half of them do not mention payroll as a service that they provide, then they probably are not a threat.. and so on.

Never believe every claim a competitor makes in their adverts and press releases as most sales and marketing people will try to stretch the truth at every opportunity they get. Once you are aware that they exist you can contact them yourself, incognito of course, for information about them and their services; or ask a friend or associate to do it for you if you think they may catch on; or try to find out by asking customers of yours who may have information about them or at least some hearsay which could help you with assessing how significant a threat they could be.

You need to know who your competitors are, so spend some time finding out, either personally or delegate it to someone you can trust.

How you deal with them is a another matter but it will be covered by many of the other chapters in this series of Ways 2 Win books.

> *Information and Communication Technology; my son David thrives on it, is totally committed to it, passionate about it and earns a living from it, which is just as well for my business. 20 years ago I used to share his enthusiasm, which encouraged him, fortunately, to do well in ICT with the result that he oversees all of our ICT requirements as Solar Solve's ICT Consultant. We are too small to need a full time ICT employee but we certainly do use Information and Communication Technology extensively.*
>
> *With an expert leading the way and a couple of other employees carrying out his directions, it works for us.*

025 - The Importance of ICT

ICT covers so many things these days. The hardware includes computers, printers, fax machines, photocopiers, scanners, telephones, laptops, servers, addressing machines, folding and envelope stuffing machines, projectors and all of the stuff I have missed out.

Then there are all of the software packages and programs that include operating systems; office suites; anti virus; anti spyware; backups; emails; internet; production processes; enquiries, quotations and orders: design packages; sales, marketing and accounts packages; and so it goes on, ad infinitum or so it seems.

Like it or not; just find it frustrating or actually hate the whole lot of it, a winning organisation won't get far without embracing it.

A few businesses still get away without using ICT but they are thin on the ground and disappearing fast. Youngsters of today give the impression they were born with push buttons, switches, remote controls and mobile phones in their hands.

It has been the way forward in my businesses since I went back to evening classes in 1980, at the age of 37, to study for my GCE 'O' level in Computer Studies so that I could write my own programs in Basic, to speed up creating price lists and customer quotations for my window blind business.

But that's what winners do. They continually look around to see what is going on and if they can use anything to their advantage. In this case my enthusiasm inspired my son. I subsequently lost interest but his enthusiasm continues to inspire the whole team at Solar Solve to be guided by him and take on board his suggestions for investing in the latest technology whenever he thinks it will benefit us.

I cannot say how important ICT is or would be for the kind of organisation you are running or intend to run but I can say that if you get the opportunity to carry out some of your processes or procedures with the help of ICT or electronic equipment you should seriously consider it. However there are at least two things you need to take into consideration. The Cost; will any effective and / or efficient benefits gained be worth the initial outlay and subsequent operating costs? The Maintenance; will you have access to an individual or supplier who can turn up at short notice and reasonable cost to sort any problems that will almost certainly crop up from time-to-time?

Important though selecting ICT equipment is, you must try to find an advisor who is not ultimately going to be a beneficiary from your equipment purchases, to guide you on the hardware or software choices so as to avoid a conflict of interest on their part.

You do not want to be persuaded to buy technology for the sake of technology, just because it is available, if you will not use it. Avoid *All Singing, All Dancing* if *Plain Ordinary* will do.

ICT is important to the vast majority of organisations as long as it is chosen carefully and considerately for the business in question, will be correctly used and maintained at an acceptable cost.

A couple of questions you may want to ask when looking to buy a piece of hardware or software are, "Will it greatly improve the service we give to our customers?" and, "Will it put us ahead of the competition?". If "Yes", then cost may not be such a major factor but the requirement that you have access to a fast and efficient ICT expert in times of difficulty almost certainly will be.

My son David, above, in the server room at Solar Solve planning out how the new computer upgrades are going to be routed round the factory.

At the risk of being accused of nepotism I wanted to include David for family reasons. He does not work full time in the family business because we do not have enough ICT equipment or demand to keep his interest in what for David is his first love. Similarly my wife Lilian has always been a very supportive partner but she does not work full time for Solar Solve and is not excited by it.

Our daughter Julie, David's twin sister, on the other hand is as enthusiastic about the business as I am and has worked full time for Solar Solve since 1991 and part time since she was about 13. We have experienced many highs and lows since 1975 but have always been very successful at keeping business and family life separate.

> *Possibly one of the greatest mistakes made by the owners of 'Ordinary' businesses that make a profit is to take out all of the profits. Whilst they are at liberty to do so, it is rarely a wise choice.*
>
> *Owners of 'Winning' businesses will firstly pay all of the tax that is due on any profits and then refer to their 3-year plans for the organisation, to establish their aims for the future, how much they have predicted the objectives will cost and where the funding is going to come from.*
>
> *It may be that it would be wise to leave all of the profits in the business, or maybe just take out a proportion of them.*

026 - Re-Invest Profits

Assuming your enterprise is making profits, then it is really a matter of what plans are in place for its future, together with your hopes and expectations regarding your financial investment.

If you are taking or being paid a salary by the business that is acceptable to you, then you are in a better position to make the right decision about profits.

As mentioned in the Intro-Box, the FIRST thing you should do is put plans in place to ensure the tax due is paid on time because the LAST thing you want to do is get into trouble with the tax authorities. They want the tax due to them and will go to extremes if necessary to get it. So in my case I just pay up, grin and bear it because there are a lot of losers out there who don't make a profit, so don't pay taxes but wish that they did. In other words why not think yourself lucky that you are a corporation tax payer, it is something to be proud of in my opinion.

Once the tax is paid out of the profits, the remainder is what you have left to dispose of. In the early years most owners of enterprising businesses will want it to grown and expand, which means that some or all of the profits should be left in the business. You may well need to borrow to set up a business or to help your business thrive and grow. However it makes no sense to borrow money that you have to pay interest on when you have made your own money that can be used to fund or part fund your business's future.

The only good thing about borrowing money is the discipline that you have to endure as you work through the borrowing process and subsequent updates the lender will insist on. This is definitely not a bad thing and because it is not necessary if you fund yourself, it can be detrimental to the business. However winners will have all sorts of procedures in place that will cover such issues and they are not likely to be of concern.

As I grew Solar Solve I needed funds to buy 3 or 4 times the volume of components normally associated with a business of my type and size, to put into stock. I was importing many of the items I needed with 50% of them having a 4 month lead time. There was the possibility I would get a big order and not have the stock to manufacture it, or that a supplier would go bust and I would run out of stock before a new supplier could be found.

The decision was easy. I needed to hold between 8 months and 12 months stock of most components in my factory. When stocks are down to 12 month levels we put in an order that takes 4 months to be delivered by which time we are at 8 months stock but the delivery brings us back up to 12 months. Straight away we put an order in for another 4 months supplies and so it goes on. We have no worries about running out of stock and with a minimum of 8 months worth of supplies it means that if a supplier goes bust we have enough time in which to find another one.

Accountants and Bank Mangers over the years have implied it is not the best use of our personal funds but it works for us because the stock and components do not go out of date, which is ideal. It also means I can sleep at nights, no problem!

Leaving profits in your business can also mean nobody is stressing you out wanting money all of the time. It helps to improve your quality of life and eventually, after reaching the size of organisation that you are aiming for, you can start to take out just about all of the profits that your business has generated after paying the tax due, of course.

Financial awareness, financial practice and financial control are crucial to business success.

If you do not have such skills when you start up a business you had better soon learn them or hire them, if your company is going to be a winner. The one good thing is that they can be fairly easily engaged and once a good accountant or financial adviser is on board, their advice should be listened to and always taken into consideration during your entrepreneurial decision making process. Ignore it at the peril of your organisation!

027 - Financial Control In All Of Its Forms

After spending almost 10 years becoming fully qualified as a Chartered Marine Engineer I took a job ashore with a multi national American organisation setting up in north east England.

My boss, who was also a professional engineer, took no time at all in advising me that whilst I would have the opportunity to do well in the company, I would never reach the top. It was his opinion that in most if not all successful organisations the person running it was either an Accountant or someone with finance and accounting skills, knowledge or understanding.

It seemed to me that whilst it may have been sarcasm or resentment on his part, he was right and ultimately, I had to become self employed to get to the top position in my own company. The irony is that whilst I made a fairly good job of running it, my failure to apply a financial discipline was holding the company back.

I eventually brought in someone with the necessary skills, who happened to be my daughter, to work with me. She advised me where I was going wrong and what we should be doing. Together we have turned a perfectly good but struggling organisation into one that is now extremely successful with an excellent financial structure. It took Julie only 18 months to have the 15 year old overdraft worked off and a further year to ensure we have always had significant cash reserves ever since.

The moral of this piece is short, simple and to the point. Unless you are well trained in the financial complexities of running a business, including turnover projections, budgets, credit control, cash flows, profit and loss accounts, balance sheets, gross profit, operating profit, net profit, overheads, capital expenditure deferred payments, dividend distribution, company tax, employee National Insurance payments, company National Insurance payments, Pay As You Earn, etc, etc, then I strongly suggest that all business owners and managers should assess the financial controls they have in place. Ask yourself if you can deal with all of the financial issues associated with you organisation to get maximum benefit for the business or should you hand them over to someone who has more knowledge and capability.

If you are struggling financially or even if you are getting along okay it may be worth having someone assess how you could do things better. There is every chance that they will identify a more effective or efficient way of doing things, which will cover their fee many fold. It could even prevent you from going bust.

In our case we converted an overdraft into a cash reserve not because Julie came in and sold more products or increased the prices. What she did was to question every item of expenditure. Could we buy it cheaper? Did we need to buy such a lot at one time? Did we need to stock so much? Can we get a discount for early payment? Can we get some customers to pay pro-forma. Why do we not send out statements? Why do we not start asking for payment immediately the 30 days are up? Do we need the heating and lighting on all day? Why do we give so many discounts when customers don't ask for them? So it went on and it was difficult at first but she persevered and eventually got everyone thinking like she does. What a difference it made.

You can get independent advice on where to find an accountant or consultant who will carry out a financial assessment for you and whether or not it can be grant assisted, by contacting your local service providers.

Just remember that financial control is absolutely vital to the success of a winning business.

There is absolutely no doubt at all, networking is wholly conducive to business success. There are numerous ways in which a business can benefit from networking just as there are various ways to network. Ultimately it is all about one or more people in any organisation making it their business to see what they can find out, what contacts they can make and how they can put the message over, that their business exists and what it has to offer.

If it is done properly, business owners and managers can benefit by establishing personal friendships, learning about advice and assistance that may well be free of charge and may even include financial support.

028 - Business Networking

Most people enjoy giving others the benefit of their experiences and get a lot of satisfaction from helping whoever they can. Effective networkers also discover how, where and to whom their organisation can target its products or services. This will not necessarily be directly to the people they talk to or their company but to some other third party target that evolved as a result of what was said during the conversation.

Networking can be done physically by attending seminars, workshops and trade association meetings where a lot more can usually be gained by talking informally with other delegates, than from the actual formal presentation itself.

Making appointments with officers of the numerous government-funded service providers can reap real benefits. Not only are they employed to help business owners and managers, which they do very well but they can usually point individuals in the direction of even more help or networking opportunities.

Effective networking can be achieved using the telephone although cold calling is very much frowned upon. However it can be a useful tool for retaining contact with someone you met personally on a previous occasion. In my organisation we ring customers and potential customers throughout the year with a courtesy call and collect a huge amount of market intelligence as a result of the conversations. Notes are always made and filed, which contain details of the call and any salient points of interest. We always ask if it is OK to ring them again at sometime in the future and more than 50% are happy to take a call as long as it is kept short and there is no sales pressure. This is fine because in this context they are part of our market research and as such prove to be very worthwhile.

In these modern technological times it is still possible to continue networking through the written word whether it is via the old-fashioned post, fax or more up to date e-mail. I'm not so sure if text messaging is considered acceptable as a means of networking although it is very useful for travel companies and dentists to remind people of arrangements and appointments.

Communicating in this way can enable a business to create the impression that it is far bigger than it actually is. There is nothing wrong with this as long as the facts are true and are just being cleverly delivered. It can be achieved by sending newsy and interesting press releases about recent events to local newspapers and trade journals. Most organisations have a least one event a month to shout about and so someone needs to be charged with turning it into an interesting news story.

Most businesses should be in a position to do all of these things yet very few tend to bother, which is great news for the ones that do. That is why all business owners and managers should be making sure that they find time to put some effort into networking for the benefit of themselves, their organisation and its employees.

They can begin by visiting a local Business Club or Rotary Club meeting where a group of local business professionals gather to discuss what is happening in their town or borough as well as within their own company. Most areas of the UK have such groups where representatives from local support agencies also attend to give advice, assistance and encouragement. Everyone benefits and there is often a buffet or tea/coffee break enabling informal networking opportunities to round it all off.

Above, the author is presented with a 'Thanks You' gift for taking part in an interview at South Tyneside Business Network, to discuss how he became the owner of a successful local business and the philosophy he applies to running it.

Becoming a member and attending Business club meetings is a great way to make contact with like-minded individuals who share the same experiences and concerns and is usually well worth the effort, though they do not work for all entrepreneurs.

The photo below was taken in 2002 and is a pretty good example of how not to network. Solar Solve sponsored the event and about 80 people were present yet this group of four all work for Solar Solve. I wonder how many useful individual networking opportunities were missed. The good news is that lessons have been learned since then and Solar Solve's employees are much more pro-active now at similar networking events, as winners need to be.

> *A winning employer and manager will ensure that systems are in place to ensure that all employees are properly managed and supervised. A lot of emphasis is placed on the managing part and a whole host of books have been written on the subject. There does not seem to be so much emphasis put on the supervision aspects of running a winning business but it is equally as important.*
>
> *As much as anything, problems arise because personnel working within an organisation may well be promoted to a Supervisor role without any formal training, as an easy option for the managers, which is rarely a good idea.*

029 - Supervision Needs Time, Inclination & Effort

The title of this chapter is aimed at the owner-manager who is doing lots of the management tasks associated with running a business all alone, with little or no help but with a few employees working alongside.

As well as managing the employees and telling them what needs to be done, they also need to be checked up on to ensure they are doing things correctly The checks need to be regular as well, at least until each individual person has proven themselves to be competent and reliable and can work with minimum supervision.

In these days of political correctness and multi discrimination laws, supervision has become a clever skill that in some organisations borders on practically being an art form because getting it wrong can be a nightmare. You will appreciate therefore, it's probably not a good idea to pick the longest serving employee and promote them whenever you need a supervisor.

Good supervision takes time, to check something thoroughly and to ensure it was produced on time, to specification and according to the laid down procedures. Remember 'Near Enough Is Not Good Enough'. This applies to tangible and intangible procedures. If an employee has to carry out any task, they should be supervised until they are signed off as being competent.

Do not think as a supervisor you will just have a quick glance to see if everything is OK as you rush by. In a winning business all supervisory checks are documented... on paper... as evidence!!

Good supervision needs the inclination and determination to do it right. There should be no half measures; no rushing in the hope that you will find everything is OK and if you don't, no temptation to turn a blind eye. If there is something wrong, you must point it out and make sure it is corrected and re-checked.

Good supervision takes a lot of effort, as you will have realised by now and if you need to supervise people who may need to be standing around some of the time (eg. sales assistants), make sure you make your mark and your point. They should be smart, always attentive and not talking to each other. The ones who resent you making an issue, if they are failing to keep up your standards, are the ones who have to be trained to understand, or dismissed if they cannot see the error of their ways.

Good supervision needs commitment, not just to carrying out the supervisory tasks already referred to, but to either converting the non-believers or having them move on.

If the owner manager is carrying out the role of supervisor, then the need to discipline employees occasionally may well be covered by another role that they are also responsible for. An employee who has been promoted to Supervisor, or employed in that role, could well be tasked with disciplining some people, at least in the early stages of a problem. They could be expected to log and monitor lateness and absence and act in some way if documented guidelines are broken. These days it is wise to include other people in all aspects of the disciplinary procedure, as the issues could be a mine field and are just another reason why Supervisors need to be selected carefully and well trained to do the job required of them.

If you are covering the role yourself then allow plenty of time, put in a lot of effort backed up with determination and commitment to get it right and be a winner.

> *As much as anything it is all about just 'Being There'. If you cannot be there then at least be available and show an interest, there is no bigger or better motivator for your employees than for them to know you are aware of them and you appreciate what they do for your organisation.*
>
> *Motivating everyone to do as much as they can, for the benefit of your customers and the rest of the team, takes a lot of working out and implementation. I have discussed in this chapter what works for my organisation but you should know that some of them may not work for you. However, if you think and work along the same lines you should get there in the end.*

030 - Motivating Your Staff

When I first began to employ people about 30 years ago, I thought that offering them a good job, for a fair wage, should be all the incentive they need to turn up for work every day; never being late and always being enthusiastic. It was, for about the first 3 months for most of them, until apathy set in and many employees started to lose interest and enthusiasm. It is at that point I tended to become indignant and started lecturing one and all (well it was aimed at my wife actually, at home over our evening meal), about how ungrateful employees are. Surely they should realise how fortunate they are to have a job?... and so on... and so forth....

When the tirade subsided Lilian would calmly put the employees viewpoint and explain that I am motivated because it is my organisation and I benefit directly by what I do and how successfully I do it. Other members of staff have no such motivation.

Thanks to my wife, I realised the error of my ways early on and set out to devise ways to motivate employees. I must have been very successful, because for the last 20 years most of the people who joined us, but did not stay with us, either left of their own accord, or were persuaded to leave because they had the wrong attitude. They just didn't fit in with Solar Solve's work ethic.

I will list in no particular order the things we do to motivate employees and the things they do for company in return.

- Cakes/pies all round at morning break on Birthdays; at the end of a week when the sales target is reached; at the end of a month when the target set for 'Banked Income' has been reached.
- Free staff night out bowling with a meal and free drinks every quarter.
- Free Christmas party night out bowling with a Christmas meal and free drinks.
- Free Christmas meal at lunchtime on the last day of working before the Christmas holidays with free drinks and the rest of the day off.
- Extra 3 days holiday per year after 3 years service.
- Extra 6 days holiday per year after 6 years service
- Extra 9 days holiday per year after 10 years service
- Select a Star Employee every 6 months who holds the trophy for 6 months and gets an extra day's holiday.
- Staff suggestion scheme that offers monetary rewards for good ideas and is well subscribed to.
- A Goodie Bag at Christmas that is a personal 'Thank You' gift from the chairman with cash, sweets and biscuits that he buys and pays for himself, to show his appreciation for employees' commitment.
- A bonus is paid to all employees every June and December out of profits, even during the recession, with everyone receiving exactly the same amount.
- A cost of living rise for everyone is awarded at the annual Staff Appraisals in January, with performance related enhancements for people who have taken on extra responsibilities, or have been exceptional in some other way.

In return for all of these staff motivators, employees first and foremost are expected to work closely together as a team. We do have an office area and a factory production area but there is absolutely no demarcation – we all pull together for the benefit of the customer and ultimately the benefit of the company.

As a result we all reap the rewards. However the employees only get paid if they turn up for work. They are penalised if they are late for work and are not paid anything by the company if they are off sick. The government pays a minimal amount of Statutory Sick Pay.

Solar Solve's employees are rarely off sick and almost never late and they are very proud of the fact. There are 17 of us and there are often years when nobody has been late or when nobody has taken time off for sickness.

There have been years when nobody was late, or off sick and quite a few people have never been late in 2, 5, 7, 10 and 17 years.

A couple of long serving employees have never been off sick.

I am not claiming we are unique by any means but these facts and figures are what a winning enterprise is all about. This is what you have to strive for if you want to be amongst the best in the world and hopefully you do.

Continuing with the 'What is expected from employees' thread, you need to know that all of our products are tailor made. We cannot manufacture anything to stock on shelves ready for orders to come in. If an order comes in today that is required in Rotterdam tomorrow morning we have to make it within whatever time is left of today because we have a 'fast turnaround – rapid response' philosophy. It may entail working during lunch or break times to catch the carriers van. Everyone will work and take their break when the rush is over – there is never a problem with it, at all, from anyone. We are all happy to take on the challenges and to have the work. We know the world doesn't owe us a living.

Many employees have taken on roles and responsibilities they didn't expect they would be doing when they joined the company. Excluding the founders, half of our employees have been with the company for 9 years or more. Once they join the team the people with the right attitude don't want to leave and we don't want them to go. The same thing should happen for you.

> *In a winning organisation within weeks of a new employee being taken on, some form of training schedule will be underway. The training can be in many forms and for many reasons. It might be a huge organisation that needs to be learnt about in general, or one that has special ways of doing things, like dangerous products or special procedures.*
>
> *They may want everyone to be trained first aiders, or go through a company Health and Safety course.*
>
> *It could be that whilst a new employee has the basic skills or qualifications, they need to be honed for their new job role.*
>
> *Or they may have been hired simply because they have the right attitude and all of the skills they need will be learned through training and on-the-job experience.*

031 - Good Staff Training Is Absolutely Essential

When a winning Enterprise is being checked out by an external auditor, they can tell a lot about it from the Financial Statements and not just the turnover and how profitable it is.

Other figures they will be looking for are the annual Research and Development budget and the annual Training budget. It all harps back to the Quality Assurance aspect of Documentary Evidence. I have been an observer on audits where both questions have been posed about how much R&D / Training has been done and the verbal answers are invariably, "Ah! Oh! Yes we do lots of R&D and Training.". When the auditor checked the figures however, there was only a couple of hundred pounds spent on each in the previous year and the auditee wasn't able to come up with much in the way of training records or research documents.

The winning way forward regarding staff training is not to accept that it is necessary; but to realise that it is going to be vital to your business as a way of improving it. You do not have to sit down and draw up all of the Staff Training plans yourself but whichever way it is done, make sure you personally are included in it for two reasons. To improve your own skills and abilities and to send a message to other employees that you believe in it yourself.

Where I live, there are many training organisations that are more than happy to visit businesses and other organisations, to review their training needs and either arrange to do the training where they can, or to advise where suitable training can be found if they are unable to do it themselves.

Some of the training organisations are government backed or receive government or local authority funding and may be able to offer free or grant-assisted courses, whilst others are private and charge quite a lot in some cases, yet they seem to survive very well.

We use St. John's Ambulance and the British Red Cross for our First Aid training courses and the company that services our Fire Fighting equipment for a bit of basic fire fighting, because some people never get to set off a fire extinguisher let alone put a controlled fire out with it. Many local Fire Brigades also provide courses and training facilities.

In the true style of winners, we adopt a Quality Assurance Standard for Solar Solve's Staff Training. It is structured and applied individually during a discussion between the employee and the manager responsible. The suggestions are then discussed by the board for approval, to confirm the training will be beneficial to the employee and the company and that the cost is acceptable.

Every employee has a Staff Training Record which lists all of the skills and training they will need from the day they start working for the company. There is a start date and a completion date, which is the day they are signed off as being competent. During the training period they are not allowed to work on production tasks unsupervised.

All of this is documented and traceable not just for the benefit of an auditor but because it is the right way to do it, especially when the employee is being Appraised. There are no misunderstandings about their training, it is all there and makes life easy for everyone, and each employee is responsible for ensuring their own personal Training Record is up-to-date.

Staff Reviews or Staff Appraisals take place for the benefit of both employee and employer. They are another stride forward from the old days when nobody was praised, everybody was criticised, your meagre pay increase was given grudgingly and you were sacked on the spot if your face didn't fit. Happy days! I don't think so, having been there myself, although as an employer, I sometimes get frustrated about the fact that I cannot dismiss someone that is obviously not good for my company, the one I built up with a lot of hard work over many years, without jumping through hoops. Such is life and I have now come to appreciate and embrace Staff Appraisals.

032 - Performance Reviews – Your Employees

Performance reviews of the organisation, referred to in chapter 36, may tend to take place quite regularly and rightly so, whereas performance reviews of employees may only need to take place annually and would probably include a salary review as well.

My winning organisation has two kinds of Employee Performance review. The first one is where the Agenda Item is *Overview of Staff Performance* and it occurs on three agendas every month; the monthly Managers Meeting, Divisional Directors Meeting and Board Meeting. The purpose of these is to assess if there have been any issues with staff members misbehaving, being unable to perform properly, being persistently late or sick and of course which people have performed particularly well or have achieved something special during the month.

Because of confidentiality issues and because we do not want to be accused of berating someone without just cause, we have to cover the issue 3 times every month as there are people in the Managers meeting we discuss at the Divisional Directors meeting and then a person at the DD meeting we discuss at the board meeting. It is long winded but it works for us and is worth the repetition because we have virtually no problems in this regard.

I keep repeating that to be a winner you have to do the things that the others just cannot be bothered with and after all of the aforesaid meetings the board knows exactly who is doing well and if there are any problems of concern. Occasionally there has been and actions were taken to resolve the issues before they grew out of proportion.

The second Employee Performance Review is what we call *Staff Appraisals* and are where the employee and his or her managers(s) meet formally to discuss or Appraise their performance.

At Solar Solve every employee has a Formal Staff Appraisal in January, when their annual salary rise is also discussed and implemented and an Informal Staff Appraisal 6 months later, in July.

We have forms that the employee fills in with their opinion about how they have performed in general, in specific ways, at specific tasks, overall and their lateness, attendance and discipline records.

These are worked through and discussions take place between the employee and the supervisor / manager / director with a view to reaching an agreement on what is good and not so good with any criticisms expected to be constructive, so that an acceptable way forward can be agreed and implemented. The agreement, which may well include an element of training, will form the basis of what will be discussed and reviewed at the next appraisal.

Management are always careful to balance their observations to include as many positive aspects as possible, so that employees do not look upon them as being witch-hunts. Employees are encouraged to ask questions and give feedback on anything they like, or don't like, about the organisation.

The Informal July meetings are documented but only to record the fact that they have taken place. For everyone involved it is just an opportunity to report back on how the employee is getting on with their January objectives and if there are any issues they want to raise.

> *Demarcation in the UK in the 1960's and 1970's was the death knell of many industries resulting in huge swathes of unemployment, the vast majority of it being self inflicted by non-cooperative workforces, who would not believe that they were on a journey of self destruction, in my opinion. Only when it was too late did the majority realise the error of their ways; a few others I think have yet to be convinced, even today, when the UK has so little manufacturing industry left. Even after the passage of up to 50 Years and the benefit of the associated hindsight, there are still some 'Die-Hards' who will never see the error of their ways, again in my opinion.*
>
> *Fortunately, for whatever reason, partly I suspect the more open-mindedness of the younger generation; the word demarcation and the act itself are now no longer an issue in most organisations.*
>
> *Today, a Multi-Skilled, Multi-Tasked, Willing Workforce is definitely the way forward for a Winning Organisation.*

033 - A Multi-Skilled, Multi-Tasked Workforce

Encouraging your employees to become multi skilled may not suit every type of organisation or some of its departments. It may not even appeal to the workforce. Persuading them to then practice multi tasking may definitely be perceived as ' a step too far'. However, business owners and managers who can take advantage of such an opportunity must give serious consideration to it, as should their workforce.

It's a very unique and fortunate organisation that has every employee turn up for work every day, happy and ready to do whatever it takes. If nothing else your staff deserve their holidays and usually that means someone has to cover for them, if the service you give to your customers is not going to suffer. Also, taking into account sickness and absence for attending training courses, means that you really should be considering how you can encourage and train existing employees to become multi skilled.

The difference between multi skilled and multi tasked is that multi skilled people are either trained in, or already possess, a variety of skills. They have the ability, but do not necessarily carry out the tasks, possibly because they are not required to or have never been asked to. Multi tasked people carry out a variety of work procedures and are usually able to ensure that the organisation functions at optimum performance at all times, because they can be moved about from one task to another to meet customer demands and are very happy to do so.

Perhaps your current practice is that some of your staff try to cover for others who are off site for whatever reason, to try and give the impression of normality. This may not be the ideal solution but it is a step in the right direction. However, the questions are: - "Are the 'stand ins' trained and qualified in the various skills?" "Does it happen in an organised fashion having been documented as an operating practice?"

In some organisations that are totally committed to multi skilling, multi tasking; some employees are rotated so that they are regularly updated and aware of the current situation surrounding their various tasks. It keeps them in tune with the procedure so that they can be up to speed on all of their skills and tasks within a very short time as the work situation dictates.

You will often find more encouragement than resistance from employees, most of whom will like the variety and interest that multi tasking offers, making their work more enjoyable and their individual value to the organisation much greater.

In my company all employees have Training Records that they must keep up to date, recording the dates training in a task began and ended, at which time they are signed off as being competent. During the training period they are not allowed to work on production tasks unsupervised. The Production Technicians are trained until they are signed off as being 'competent' to carry out all of the various production, packing and dispatch procedures, so that even if they are the only person in the factory on a particular day, at least any urgent orders can be made and dispatched by just one person. The chances are some of the people in the office will be competent to work in the factory as well.

Skilled Production Technicians are encouraged to train in some of the office procedures that may include dealing with Enquiries, Quotations and Order Processing, various marketing activities and other computer based tasks.

The longer serving employees, or ones with special skills are the Trainers at the regular In-house training sessions covering production, installation and administration skills and techniques. They regularly receive training lectures themselves from external trainers and know exactly how to prepare beforehand and present the sessions in a professional manner. Employees are encouraged to take on various other responsibilities such as Health and Safety, Fire Wardens, Uniforms Officer, Social Secretary being just a few. They are also encouraged to attend external First Aid courses to become Certified First Aiders.

Some of the responsibilities may not seem to be very important but in a highly organised kinetic enterprise it saves a lot of time if people know exactly who to go to for the item or assistance that they are looking for. They know it will be from someone in their team who is adept at the task and can complete it quickly for them or with them.

There was an occasion at the end of 2008 when we were so busy at Solar Solve that even with overtime we were not going to get all of the orders out on time and so I volunteered to operate the chop-saw. It was agreed but only under supervision because my Training Record did not show me as 'Competent'. I had been competent many years previously but had let most of the practical tasks on my Training Record lapse. That said, we still got everything out first time, on time, every time, for the customer; as winning businesses do, but it was 'touch-and-go' on that occasion.

This is an opportunity to repeat what I wrote in Chapter 30. As much as anything it is all about just 'Being There'. If you cannot be there then at least be available and show an interest, there is no bigger or better motivator for your employees than the boss being around and being involved.

This subject can be a contentious one, because I have always believed in leading by example and am more than happy to come into work and clean the loos if we are getting a high profile visitor and everyone else is busy doing more important tasks, especially if they are dealing with customers, who come first, last and everywhere in between, in a winning between.

034 - Leading From The Front

As the chairman of the Board of Directors of a company (it does not matter what we produce or how big we are) my primary role and legal responsibility is to lead and direct the company.

If I was the senior partner in the corner sweet shop or the manager or the sole owner, my primary role would not legally be the same. I could choose not to lead and direct and if I was the manager, working for a large group, I would probably not be required to lead and direct to that level. However, in all of the cases mentioned , as the senior member of staff I should certainly be leading from the front, or at least be prepared to do so when necessary, whether it was a legal requirement or not.

For the readers who are leaders and have opted to take a bit of a back seat because they have delegated much of their day-to-day work successfully, then it will be a case of "Well Done!" but you are still the leader, a role that cannot normally be delegated, otherwise you would be extraneous to requirements. It is a mistake for those leaders who delegate to think that they have solved the problem and all will be well in future.

It is human nature for people to work better and more effectively when they are motivated and there is no better motivation than knowing your boss is going to be checking up on you occasionally. The only way the leader can perform that task properly is to get out and about amongst the troops (even if it is just one other person) to find out what is and isn't happening and then address any issues as soon as possible. Don't wait until they are reported back to you because a lot of them won't be. It is also human nature to cover your mistakes if you think you will get away with it. A mistake made by an employee could result in an unhappy customer and could have happened before and maybe will happen again. Unhappy customers are not good news and generally vote with their feet, going straight to your competitor.

If you don't take an interest through an inquiring mind there are lots of things you will miss. Leading is certainly telling people what you want them to do. Showing them how it needs to be done if necessary. Giving them deadlines in which to do it, always being careful to stipulate that the deadlines are flexible if they need to do something for a customer who is waiting for an order to be completed. Customers come first in winning enterprises.

As leader you have lots of responsibilities that include:
- Decision Making
- Execution of Plans (you don't have to create the plans but you will have to see them brought to fruition)
- Organisation
- Supervision
- Many other issues related to Quality Assurance, Health and Safety, Sales and Marketing, Financial Control.

You need to be sure that you have competent people covering all of these functions. In a small business it may be the same person doing all of them. Never mind as long as they get done and get done properly. Just going through the motions is absolutely no use to anyone, you might as well not bother because you will get caught out sooner or later.

If it is a winning organisation you are after, you cannot fool systems because the ultimate monitor is how well you do, how well your organisation performs out there in the real world. YOU don't declare yourself to be a winner, the people you serve are the judges, so YOU HAVE TO DO IT RIGHT TO WIN.

Another one of the main requirements for any organisation to become a winner is to have at least one person responsible for leading and directing it. In fact the best option is to have only one person at the helm; then, depending on its size, that person will be closely supported by capable and effective deputies. For Limited Liability companies it could be a Chairman who is supported by a board of directors. A one-person Limited Company will probably do everything and take the title of Managing Director whereas if it is not incorporated the person may be called 'Owner' or 'Partner'. Whatever the circumstances the person in charge should not forget to Lead and Direct as well as also doing a whole lot of other things.

035 - Directing Your Organisation To Success

Whether or not your organisation is incorporated as a Public or Private Limited Company or simply a firm that trades as a sole ownership or a partnership, it is going to need someone to successfully lead and direct it towards its stated objectives.

This chapter is not about the Legal aspects and responsibilities of those people who opt to take on a title and role as Director. There are plenty of books already written on the subject and it is worth reading some of them if you are, or intend to be, a Company Director, to clarify what duties you are expected to perform and what is required of you legally.

Nor can I give advice on the best option for your organisation regarding which type of enterprise to create. Limited liability companies are best suited for some organisations whereas simple 'firms' are fine for others. You should discuss this with an accountant before you set up a business, or if you are already in business your accountants will be only too pleased to give you their advice and explain the differences between the two.

I started in business in 1975 as a simple partnership with my wife. It was perfectly adequate for a town centre shop. Then in 1988 we decided to reinvent ourselves which involved selling to the marine industry world wide and so we converted to a Ltd. Co.

When I first started in business I kept myself to myself and simply supplied my customers with their wants and needs for the first 13 years or so. I didn't network in any direction, in any way. Nothing ever occurred to me that I was running a business and I needed to market it. After all, I had a shop on the high street and thought that was all I needed. When I realised it was not enough I put ads in the local evening paper. It helped but was costly so by accident I got some work from the council in schools and offices. Probably from an advert but I hadn't gone looking for it. I was an ex Marine Engineer who had blundered in to the window blind business because I wanted to be self employed and thought that buying a high street business and giving a good service was all that was needed. I was so Naïve it's a wonder I survived for as long as I did.

Then, just before I was about to go bust because of my inability to sell enough blinds, I got the chance to make special blinds for ships. I eventually saw the opportunities and somehow started to network, by going to council business events and meeting other self employed people who were just like me. I listened to the speakers giving advice on all kinds of things like Quality Assurance, grant assistance, marketing graduates at £10 a week for 6 months and my business life and attitude changed.

The re-invention at that time, from Northern Window Blind Company to Solar Solve Ltd trading as Solar Solve Marine was spectacular. We changed from the safety of a proven range of products sold to the public and commercial offices, to a new product that I had designed and manufactured, which was targeted at the global marine industry.

To do that, not only did I have to find out all about the complications of exporting, I had to import the major components for the new products because they were not available in the UK.

The offer of the cut-price marketing graduate came just at the right time and proved to be very beneficial. That was when I realised that if I was going to be successful I needed to employ people, I was never going to make it with just my wife and family working with me. It seems silly now but I still did not realise I needed to plan what I was doing and what I was going to do and how I was going to get there. I had done a 3-page document for the bank manager explaining that I was changing tack, re-branding etc., and would need a bigger overdraft, which didn't impress him and he didn't bite. I had not included any cash flow figures, because I didn't really know what they were. My accountant eventually helped me out with that.

When I realised that Solar Solve was going to be a somewhat different operation to the window blind shop I decided to sit down and plan out my objectives. I was meeting people in the marine industry I could learn from. I was going to the regional Blindmakers association meetings that I had always been eligible to attend, but had never bothered to and I started learning a whole lot from the other blindmakers. So I was quickly acquiring relevant knowledge that would stand me in good stead but it needed to be structured and presented logically.

As I learnt, it became obvious there were lots of strings to this new bow, some of them I was already doing, like manufacturing roller blinds, albeit simple ones and many I was not; such as Exporting, Importing, Mission Statements, Planning, Financial Control and all of the other subjects referred to in this book. I took them all on board and implemented them, with lots more learned and added to the repertoire as we continued to be more and more successful.

Although I was still fire-fighting with the day-to-day problems of selling, ordering, production, paying bills and the like, I was taking time out to network, to learn about marketing from the graduate and how to plan, lead and direct. I was always the leader, the problem had been that I didn't know where I was going and I was not taking enough time to rectify the problem with better planning. Once I did know, I made sure everyone else knew as well, so we could all pull-together. We did and I have never looked back.

So be sure you always take time out to personally direct your organisation to success and to becoming a winning enterprise.

After 20 years of dedication to the task, I now have at Solar Solve a team of people who can run the business on a daily basis without any input from me. But I still go to work on Tuesdays and Thursdays because I enjoy it and I am still full of ideas to take the company forward into the future, beyond the day-to-day routine. I also think it is important for employees to see that I am interested in what they do and impressed at how well they do it. The photo below shows me taking part in a Skyped meeting from my holiday home in Florida, which we no longer have due to grand children arriving on the scene. Note I am wearing my uniform shirt and tie to maintain the image and to lead by example. It's what I would expect others to do in similar circumstances.

In May 2011 the Solar Solve team celebrated Carl Johnson's 10 years service and Julie Lightfoot's 20 years service with the company (above) and in October 2011 they enjoyed another party to celebrate Leanne Reilly's and Paul Hopkins's 10 years of service (below). As far as John Lightfoot, the company's founder and chairman is concerned, the Solar Solve team are part of his extended family.

A Winning Organisation will be reviewing its performance regularly – daily, weekly or monthly, depending on the product or service it provides. If I was running a medical or veterinary surgery I would be wanting to know how well it was performing at the end of every day, with more detailed reviews taking place on a monthly basis.

For other businesses a monthly review will probably suffice because they will have, or should have, formal procedures in place to record individual situations where something has gone wrong and will already be working on putting them right without waiting for the regular reviews.

036 - Performance Reviews – Your Organisation

At the regular Organisation Performance Reviews you should be taking into account anything irregular that happened during the day-to-day running of the organisation since the last review. It should also include:

- Formally recorded Non Conformities of whatever type.
- Customer comments be they commendations or complaints, verbal or written.
- Any customer feedback forms that have been received.
- Any staff performance issues.
- Any supplier performance issues.

So that you end up with a general overview of how your organisation is performing overall.

If you are a business that carries out life-saving procedures and opt to take up my suggestion of daily performance reviews, backed up by regular formal monthly meetings with Agendas and Minutes, the daily meetings only have to be short ones to check that the day went well and there were no problems. Five minutes will probably be enough on most days and notes need only be taken if something of significance is discussed, especially if there is a resultant important decision made.

Whilst it would still be beneficial to hold reviews without

documenting them, they are otherwise pretty useless as evidence to support any issues that may arise at anytime.

Normally these days the attitude of all inspectors is that if it is not documented in written format, either on paper or electronically, then it simply didn't happen. You can argue as much as you want to about what may have happened or what may or may not have been said, but they will only accept evidence that they can see.

There are many reasons for holding the reviews. The best one is that your business will improve dramatically if you carry them out properly. Don't just hold a review and discover something went wrong, then discuss the reasons, say "Ah! Well, that was bad luck. Let's hope it doesn't happen again.", and move on. There will be times, albeit few and far between, when no corrective action can be taken, but 9 times out of 10 there will be something you can do about things going wrong, whether they are your organisation's fault or someone else's.

So for every issue raised you need to assess what happened that was wrong, how it happened, who or what caused it to happen and what corrective action can be put in place to ensure it does not happen again. It is definitely NOT about finding fault or apportioning blame. It IS all about putting systems in place by maybe using alternative suppliers, components or more probably just tweaking things a bit here or there to put everything right.

You're still not quite there yet though. To be absolutely sure you got it right and the problem can be signed off as having been resolved, you need to go back at a later date, or after the next time that process is used and make sure it was completed with no recurrence of the original problem.

Non Conformity Reports, Customer Feedback Forms and many other documents that are necessary to help you become a winner, will be referred to again in chapters that relate to Quality Assurance in Book 3, entitled *"40 Ways 2 Win At Exporting"*.

In the meantime you need to also Review all of your Reviews.

Reviews of all types are useful to any organisation as long as they are effective. It is not enough just to go through the process of carrying out all sorts of reviews. They need to be monitored to record what the outcome of the review was. What actions were considered necessary? Were they put into effect? Did they change the situation? How did they change it? Were any problems resolved and was the outcome of the review successful? Did nothing change and therefore an alternative strategy was discussed and implemented?

037 - Review The Reviews

To the small business owner / manager it seems that new legislation, layers of red tape and political correctness keeps bombarding their organisation from all ends and sides, taking up far too much of their valuable time.

Why then would they want to even read about suggestions for running a better business, let alone consider or adopt them?

Organisations that take time to look at themselves and to review how well they perform and then act on the findings are the ones most likely to succeed at becoming a winning enterprise.

Much of the red tape has to be complied with for many reasons, including Health and Safety. There is no legislation to insist a business analyses itself to see if it is performing effectively and efficiently (and also profitability if that is an objective).

It is unbelievably a fact that many organisations therefore choose not to analyse what they are doing or how well they are doing it, unless they have gone along the path of Quality Assurance, but more about that in another book in this series.

As well as all of the necessary reviews associated with Health and Safety and similar subjects, there should be all sorts of other reviews taking place; some annually and some more regularly.

Staff performance and salary reviews should take place

annually with a mid term performance review after 6 months.

Departmental effectiveness reviews of the Management, Technical, Production, Finance, Sales, Marketing and Administration Teams should all take place during the monthly meetings, with extensive analysis, resulting in corrective action if necessary, being done on a quarterly basis. If you do not have a meeting at least once a month for each of the functions within your business then you should be asking yourself or your management team, "Why?"

A performance and effectiveness review of the Board should be carried out annually, as should reviews of all the other departments, together with a management meeting to review the quality system if one is in place, with Minutes being issued for all.

Do not use or accept from others the excuse that daily / weekly / monthly meetings are a 'waste of time' and everyone is 'too busy' doing more urgent work. This easy option has been used for years by people in companies that can only dream of winning, but it is very unlikely that they ever will.

Once a meeting is convened make very sure that the Agenda is not just read through with everyone "Yessing" and nodding their heads in approval that all is well; with the totally unacceptable objective of "Let's get this over with as quickly as possible."

I bet that once you start asking a few searching questions it will be amazing what transpires regarding things that have gone wrong, stuff not being ordered, production and administration staff not communicating, stuff not checked and lots of other things you took for granted not getting done. Trust me on this.

And finally of course, the subject of this chapter. The Directors and Managers should meet to Review the Reviews annually to ensure they are effective, otherwise everyone could be wasting their time. When effectively applied, these guidelines will automatically make a big difference to the success of any organisation.

Long gone are the days when workers were expected to work without adequate equipment or training to protect them from hazards.

Unfortunately due to ignorance and naivety all round, the vast majority were quite prepared and even readily accepted that the risks associated with a task, trade or profession were just part of the job.

Times have changed and whilst some business owners complain about too much legislation, it must be agreed that for the most part things have changed for the better, due to the introduction and monitoring of strict Health and Safety laws.

038 - Health And Safety

Most of the current Health and Safety legislation has been long overdue and as a business owner or manager you must ensure that you organisation complies with all aspects of it, as it affects your business. If there is found to be a breach of these laws at any time, then you and / or some other senior executive within your organisation can receive heavy personal fines, imprisonment or both, depending on the seriousness of the violation.

All organisations, not just companies and businesses, should have carried out Risk Assessments for all areas of the establishment; office, factory, front shop, back shop, warehouse, whatever areas you work in, including every site visited if you carry out tasks as a subcontractor.

Once the risks have been assessed you need to make plans to eliminate them or reduce them as much as possible by issuing personal protective equipment (PPE) for example.

It is vital that you seek advice about Health & Safety and Risk Assessment – one successful compensation claim against your organisation could result in a hefty financial penalty, as well as the possibility of fines or imprisonment imposed by the courts.

Your local Business Support Agency or many of the other Business service providers will usually give you free initial advice on the complexities of the legislation.

If you have the opportunity, it can be a good idea to ask one of your employees to take on the role and additional responsibility of becoming your organisation's 'Health and Safety Officer', if the business is not big enough to warrant a dedicated person employed for that purpose.

I did and it has worked extremely well with the volunteer being sent on a few courses and gaining the necessary skills, knowledge and certificates to ensure we have created a safe and secure environment in which we can all operate virtually accident free. He has also been trained to formally identify Risk Assessments and carry out RA checks annually; spread over the four quarters.

The Health and safety Officer attends the monthly Technical / Production Meeting where any issues he raises are discussed and usually implemented for the benefit of us all.

There are a variety of Training Courses available covering all aspects of Health & Safety and Risk Assessment. Some of them may be Grant Assisted or subsidised so it is worth investigating what is available in your area. To give best support to our H&S Officer both the Operations Director and myself have attended courses to better understand the issues and what is expected of him in this important role. He knows he has our total support.

I agree that there are many instances of too much Health and Safety legislation, due to the current compensation culture of a few who tend to be spoiling it for the many. However we all deserve to be protected from the everyday risks of accidents caused by trips and slips, other hazards and lack of available PPE for example. It's good that some of the sillier rules have either been formally withdrawn or have been sidelined by default, allowing common sense to prevail.

It is all about being reasonable and applying common sense, so make it your objective to ensure that your organisation has carried out its legal duties and commitments towards Health and Safety for all of its stakeholders.

It is quite un-nerving to discover just how many organisations do not have a Disaster Recovery Plan in place. For small businesses it is probably understandable. A lot of work is needed to produce one and they will not have the manpower or finances to put one in place, opting to gamble that nothing will ever go wrong as the alternative. This subject will be covered in some detail in another book but in the meantime for the owner/manager gamblers who do not even have minimal alternative plans or systems in place, to cover for failure of suppliers or other service providers, here are a few logical pointers to take you beyond Plan 'A'.

039 - Plan 'B's – For When Things Go Wrong

If you lead or manage an organisation you should have a plethora of Plan 'B's; alternative actions that you can take when things go wrong and trust me, they will certainly be times when things go wrong.

There may be organisations that are so well run or so predictable that nothing ever goes wrong or varies from the norm, but I've yet to hear of one.

In actuality common sense should prevail. As well as Plan B's you should also have a Plan 'C' and sometimes Plans 'D E & F' if human lives depend on the outcome, or safety is an issue.

"What if?" Questions should be asked regarding all sorts of processes and procedures involved in an organisation. You should have alternative suppliers, at least for your main purchases, possibly all your purchases if they are all crucial to effective operation.

- How do you cope with staff shortages, do you just deliver everything later and if so, is that acceptable to customers?
- Would overtime cover the problem?
- What if 2 or 3 employees fail to turn in?
- What if your carrier/delivery vehicle breaks down – do you have another firm/vehicle you can call on immediately?

- What if a supplier cannot deliver on time?

It is not all about problems with suppliers, sub-contractors or service providers. There are many other circumstances that can have an influence on you organisation. Terrorism for example can have devastating effects. Thousands of organisations went out of business as a result of 9-11. Hundreds of thousands survived though because they had effective emergency plans in place, or were quick witted enough to react successfully to the problems it caused; which were significant for some types of industry.

It was a dramatic loss of sales that affected most organisations and for many, including my business, a significant drop in selling prices was the only way forward and out of the crisis.

Terrorism is probably a bit of a drastic example but I'm sure there are lots of organisations that are now well prepared for any future dramatic events that could be caused as a result of incidents like 9-11 and some more recent atrocities.

So it goes on. How do you keep secondary suppliers and service providers happy to work for you at a moments notice – but only occasionally? They are unlikely to give you an excellent service if called upon maybe just once or twice a year, if that.

The usual tactic is to give them an occasional order they can quite adequately handle and provide you with a good service, but at a higher price than you would normally pay.

A winning organisation would accept this occasional extra cost as part of its effective and efficient back-up strategy.

Finally all of the information relating to alternative suppliers and strategies needs to be well documented, kept up to date and discussed on a regular basis. Just in case you or the employee(s) with the information in their heads, don't turn up for work on the day it all goes wrong.

You know it makes sense!

I must admit that for many years I ran a business and was totally oblivious to the fact that there were stakeholders involved, always feeling that the business was mine (and my wife's) and mine alone.

What did it have to do with anyone else how I chose to run it? I was in charge of my own destiny... and so on.

Well that was over 30 years ago and was more acceptable at the time. In fact it was normal thinking for most self-employed people. It was probably one of the reasons why I was only just surviving. I was not networking in any way, just kept my shoulder to the wheel and worked hard at getting nowhere.

040 - Know Who Your Stakeholders Are

An organisation's stakeholders are generally referred to as any individual, group or organisation who is affected by, or contributes to, the organisation in any way.

Take some time to document who your organisation's stakeholders are. There is lots of information on the Internet about how to create a list of your stakeholders and how important they are or can be, to your business. My suggestion is that you list them into groups in the first instance and then break the groups down into sub-groups or individuals, as you will probably need to contact some of them from time to time at least.

Stakeholder Groups include:

- Owners
- Suppliers
- Customers
- Employees
- Unions
- Service Providers
- Councils and Local Government
- National Government
- Local Community
- Investors
- Creditors

For small enterprises it is unlikely that all of these groups will have an influential effect on your business but some of them surely will. Make sure you list those that are or could be most important, influential or helpful to you. Within the groups you then need to identify the individuals, organisations or other businesses that will be significant and annotate notes that indicate in what way they will be able to assist you, or any other reason why they have been highlighted. Useful stakeholders, apart from the obvious customers, suppliers and employees could be council planners, service providers who know influential people, your Member of Parliament and union leaders.

Creditors are stakeholders you will inherit by default, as soon as you buy something, until you have settled their accounts. In the normal course of running the business they will not be an issue as long as you meet your obligations towards them. However if you start to get financial problems and expect to default on some payments, the creditors who will be affected need to be told and it should be in advance if possible, to give them time to rearrange their finances. It may be they need your payment so that they can pay off one of their creditors, so you should warn them and give an indication of when you do expect to settle the debt.

Ask around the local community to find out if there are any issues with your organisation being located there. It is much better for a winning organisation to be embraced by the community in which it is located, rather than despised. You may be causing problems for someone, that are making them very angry, which could be easily resolved if you were aware of it.

If there are community related issues or even if you just want to be a good neighbour, you will find that offering to sponsor or support a local school or good cause can work wonders.

Gone are the old days of isolation and instead we have the modern days of openness and integration which the public are entitled to and that really are beneficial to everyone. So welcome the opportunity to become involved, because it is the right attitude for a winner.

MORE ABOUT THE AUTHOR

John Lightfoot was born in South Shields in North East England to Joseph and Georgina Lightfoot in 1943. Father Joe was a miner all of his working life and in the early years, right up to the early seventies mother Ena earned pin money making dresses, mainly for brides and bridesmaids, in the family home. John was the second of 3 children and whilst the family was not poor they were certainly working class, which was probably behind the inspiration and motivation that made him want more.

From a very early age he was growing vegetables in the garden to sell to his mother, converting old railway sleepers into bundles of sticks to sell round the doors. He was a butcher boy, grocer's boy, paper lad, golf caddie, bought stuff in bulk and sold the items on singly and made enough profit making jewellery at home to pay for all of his lessons and passing his driving test in 1963.

It's fair to say John was and still is motivated by earning money and that is why he chose the sea as his first career move. He was away from home for up to a year at a time but the pay was good.

To John, what is equally as important as earning good money and achieving a high-level status within the global marine industry that was undreamed of 50 years ago, is the fact that he was never a great academic when he was younger. 'Average' was  about as good as it got. He feels it is up to him to get the message out to all of the other 'Average' people in the world who want to become winners and achieve an 'above average' lifestyle, that it is eminently possible.

As John says, "There is nothing special about me, if I can do it, anyone can do it but you need to find the right people to help you ensure it all gels together and works well."

www.ingramcontent.com/pod-product-compliance
Lightning Source LLC
Chambersburg PA
CBHW071225170526
45165CB00003B/998